SAINT AUC

MW00895835

FATHER WILLIAM LOYD RYAN

PRIESTLY AND RELIGIOUS VOCATIONS
IN THE DIOCESE OF HAMILTON

A THESIS SUBMITTED IN PARTIAL
FULFILLMENT OF THE
REQUIREMENTS FOR THE DEGREE OF
HONOURS MASTER OF DIVINITY

BY

JOHN JOSEPH PERDUE

THESIS SUPERVISOR: DR. PETER MEEHAN

TORONTO, ONTARIO

OCTOBER 2013

© **John Perdue, 2013**

Contents

Chapter 3
Father Ryan and the Founding of the Sisters of
Our Lady Immaculate

Acknowledgement and Dedication

Many thanks to my thesis supervisor, Dr. Peter Meehan, whose thoughtful guidance and expertise helped to refine and focus this work. To the Sisters of Our Lady Immaculate, thank you for your prayerful support and for allowing me the privilege of looking into the heart of Father Ryan, your founder. This work was undertaken for you, but has benefitted me greatly.

This thesis is dedicated to Mrs. Mary Alleene Theresa Clare and to Sister St. Henry Moloney (1917 – 2013), women of great faith who are dear to Father Ryan and to me.

Introduction

One hears a great deal, in the Catholic world today, about a shortage of vocations. Some would be interested to learn, therefore, that recent statistics show a global increase in absolute number of vocations to the priesthood and to religious life. But fears of a "vocation crisis" are not unfounded when one looks at trends in North American and European figures, where the pinch of a vocations shortage has indeed been felt.[1] In the face of this shortage, it is helpful to look to examples of programs or individuals who have had success in promoting vocations to the priesthood and to religious life. In the context of the Canadian Catholic Church, one such individual was Father William Loyd Ryan (1917-2003), a priest of the Hamilton Diocese in Ontario from 1940 to 2003. By many accounts, he was a holy and faith-filled man who, among many other accomplishments,

---

[1] The 2013 Pontifical Yearbook recorded a global increase in absolute numbers of diocesan and religious priests over the past decade, despite a decrease of 9% in Europe and stable numbers in America. The number of professed women religious decreased 10% in the period from 2001 to 2011, despite an increase of 28% in Africa and 18% in Asia. "2013 Pontifical Yearbook: Permanent Diaconate Booms in Europe, U.S.," News.Va: The Vatican Today, last modified May 13, 2013, accessed July 20, 2013, http://www.news.va/en/news/2013-pontifical-yearbook-permanent-diaconate-booms.

successfully fostered and supported the vocations of many young men and women in the Diocese of Hamilton.

Under Father Ryan's prayerful guidance and encouraged by his priestly example, dozens of young men flocked to the seminary from the parishes in which he was stationed. Many went on to become priests and bishops – one to become Cardinal Archbishop of Toronto. And that's not all. Father Ryan's great love for religious life drove him to action when faced with the alarming exodus from religious life that marked the 1960s and 1970s. Supported by hours of prayer, by his Ordinary, and by the assistance of several like-minded friends, Father Ryan began the process of founding the Sisters of Our Lady Immaculate, a new women's religious community who would reside at his parish, the Church of Our Lady in Guelph. Mother Mary Josephine Mulligan would answer his call, the first of dozens of women whose vocations would be influenced by Father Loyd Ryan.

Father Ryan's awareness of the importance of religious identity was the locus of his success in fostering vocations to the priesthood and to consecrated religious life. For Ryan, to be a priest was to be an *alter Christus*, a mediator between God and humanity, called to bring souls to the Father through the Sacraments. The consecrated religious, on the other hand, was called to be the bride of Christ, conforming herself ever more closely to Him through her vows of poverty, chastity and obedience. It would take the significant ecclesiastical changes brought about by the Second Vatican Council (1962-1965) to manifest Ryan's strong priestly identity and his distinct image of consecrated religious life. In the wake of Vatican II there was relative uncertainty and confusion about what it meant to be a priest and how the ministerial priesthood differed from the priesthood of the laity. Consecrated religious, too, underwent a period of unrest as they sought to redefine their congregations according to Magisterial guidelines. The change in backdrop from black-and-white theological principals and unquestioned hierarchical obedience to a milieu of subjectivity, subsidiarity and the questioning of authority brought into relief the strong priestly identity and the strong image of consecrated religious life that Ryan had fostered during his thoroughly Catholic upbringing and rigorous seminary formation. Add to this Ryan's stubborn Irish Catholic nature and one can see why he was grounded enough in his priestly identity to weather this period of tumult. And this attracted attention. Now, given the new backdrop, Father Ryan's image of the priesthood and of consecrated religious life stood out. Young men saw in him the groundedness that they desired for their own priestly vocations, and young women were drawn to Ryan's vision of consecrated religious life and to the community he founded, the Sisters of Our Lady Immaculate.

In the 1940s and 1950s, golden years for the Roman Catholic priesthood in North America, Father Ryan, like other Catholic priests of the era, enjoyed universal respect and admiration. During these years, the young men who entered the seminary under his influence were attracted to his human qualities: his love of sports, his propensity to laugh and joke, and his generosity in inviting groups of young men to his family farm for camping and fishing trips. Father Ryan allowed the human side of his priesthood to shine through at a time when the humanity of the priest was underemphasized, with the result that he was somewhat of a hero to the local boys. Interestingly, though, after the Second Vatican Council, the young men who were influenced by Father Ryan do not point to his friendliness or his playfulness as factors that attracted them. They point, rather, to the transcendent aspects of his priestly ministry. They recognized that Ryan was a man of prayer, who deeply revered the Mass and time spent in adoration of the Blessed Sacrament. Ryan's balanced, incarnational approach to his ministry allowed both his human traits and his divine mission to be manifest; the former played a pivotal role in fostering vocations before the Second Vatican Council and the latter was in the forefront after the Council. A shift can also be noted in Father Ryan's relationship to women religious. Before the Second Vatican Council, Father Ryan enjoyed close relationships with many religious sisters, serving as chaplain to some congregations, offering the Mass for them and providing them with spiritual direction. After the Council, though, Ryan was perturbed about the direction that some women's religious orders were headed in their efforts at renewal. He believed that certain fundamental aspects of consecrated religious life were being jettisoned without sufficient discernment. Likeminded young women responded when he made an effort to found a new religious congregation that would preserve the elements of religious life that he considered essential.

Father Ryan was very clear about what things were essential to preserving his identification with the priesthood of Jesus Christ – the things that were essential to who he was. He felt that he had been consecrated a priest in order to sanctify the people of God through the Sacraments, primarily the Eucharist. He had a clear notion, too, of the means by which he would maintain and deepen this priestly identity; by fostering a devotion to the Blessed Sacrament; by offering the Holy Sacrifice of the Mass worthily; and by increasing his devotion to the Blessed Virgin Mary and the saints. Father Ryan also thought that the identity of consecrated religious would be maintained and deepened only through the evangelical counsels. For the faithful living out of the vows of poverty, chastity and obedience, he saw a need for a joyful community life centered on the Eucharist, a structured life of prayer in imitation of the Blessed Virgin Mary and a shared charism, together with external manifestations of the commitment to religious life, such as the habit.

The elements of priestly and religious life listed above may seem anything but 'visionary' to some readers. To some, they are time-tested means of communion with Christ. But remember that Father Ryan's ministry spanned a time of tremendous experimentation in religious life and priestly ministry in North America. Knowingly or not, priests in the 1960s and 1970s were testing whether their ministry would survive with a lessened emphasis on Eucharistic adoration, the Mass and external devotions; religious orders were doing the same in regard to abandoning the habit, community prayer or a communal charism. Father Ryan's steady awareness of who he was and what it meant to be a religious enabled him to weather a stormy period in priestly ministry and to foster vocations to religious life when many young women were put off by the apparent inconstancy of the vocation. He is a rare example of a priest who successfully fostered vocations both before and after the Second Vatican Council. And this influence in fostering vocations flowed from his firm awareness of the centrality of religious identity in pastoral ministry.

This analysis of the life and example of Father Ryan will provide priests, religious and laity with an example of 'what works' – what can be done to foster vocations to the priesthood and to religious life in post-secular North America. Insight into the life and work of Father Ryan will also serve as an encouragement to any who doubt that God continues to call men and women to give themselves entirely to Him. God continues to inspire new movements and foundations in His Church, and Father Ryan was an instrument in one such endeavour.

At the time of writing, many people who personally knew Father Ryan were still alive. Notable among them is Mrs. Mary Alleene Theresa Clare, Father Ryan's sister. She and Ryan's remaining friends, parishioners, family members and fellow clergymen were invaluable fonts of information. The archives of the diocese of Hamilton and of the Sisters of Our Lady Immaculate (the order that Father Ryan co-founded) contained helpful information, as did the archives of Father Ryan's parishes and seminaries. Several small parochial and regional histories also contained helpful information. Histories of Catholic education in Ontario and of the Roman Catholic priesthood and consecrated religious life since the Second Vatican Council were used to situate Ryan's life and ministry within the developing historiography of the twentieth century Canadian Church. Taken together, the information in these resources creates a picture of Father Ryan's life and ministry and his role in fostering vocations in the diocese of Hamilton.

Chapter 1

Father William Loyd Ryan (1917 – 2003)

Early Life in North Brant, Bruce County, Ontario

William Loyd Ryan[2] was born June 3, 1917 at
the Ryan family farm on the fourteenth concession of
North Brant in Bruce County, Ontario. He was the
third of seven children born to William Joseph Ryan
and Amelia Wehenkel.[3] The other children, in order of
birth, are Daniel Edmund, Frank, Philip, Mary, Lucille
and Bernice. Loyd's grandfather, Daniel Edmund
Ryan, and grandmother, Honora (Dora) Quirk, had
purchased the farm and moved there from nearby
Kinkora.[4] The farm is located a quarter of a mile down
the road from St. Michael's Church, which functioned

---

[2] Ryan's birth certificate reads 'William Lloyd Ryan,' as do
the documents pertaining to his admission to seminary and
to Holy Orders. His tombstone, however, reads 'William
Loyd Ryan.' In response to the question 'Is there one 'L' or
two?' his sister, Mrs. Mary Clare, assures that there is only
one. As she puts it, "they beat the 'L' out of him a long
time ago" (Mary Clare, interview by John Perdue,
Goderich, ON, November 21, 2009, recording in the Sisters
of Our Lady Immaculate Archives, henceforth *SOLIA*).
Whenever Ryan signed a letter, he used one 'L.' Out of
deference to him, therefore, he shall henceforth be referred
to as 'Loyd.'
[3] For an account of an interesting but unconfirmed story
from Loyd's childhood, see Appendix A.
[4] St. Michael's Church: North Brant, Ontario 1883-1983.
[Hamilton]: 1983, 99.

for many years as a mission of Sacred Heart Church in Walkerton. This is the church where Loyd was baptized on the day of his birth by Father (later Monsignor) Reuben M. Haller.[5] It is also the Church where Loyd would later celebrate his First Solemn Mass.[6]

Mrs. Mary Fleming, a long-time friend of the Ryan family, recalls the reason Loyd was given his name. Loyd's father, William, was an interested follower of local, national, and international news. Being of Irish heritage, 'Bill' had been very happy to read, in 1916, about efforts by England's Prime Minister, Daniel Lloyd George, to reconcile Unionist and Nationalist Irish and establish a system of self-governance.[7] Bill's strong patriotic loyalties led him to name his next child 'William Lloyd' - *William* after himself, and *Lloyd* after Prime Minister Daniel Lloyd

---

[5] Fr. Haller was associate pastor at Sacred Heart Church in Walkerton from 1913-1917 (St. Michael's Church: North Brant, Ontario 1883-1983. [Hamilton]: 1983, 89). This information was obtained from a copy of Ryan's Baptismal Certificate, SOLIA.

[6] "Ordination on Sunday Next: Father Lloyd Ryan of North Brant Will Celebrate First Mass in Home Parish on Sunday, the 16th of June," *The Chesley Enterprise*, June 6, 1940.

[7] David W. Savage, "The Attempted Home Rule Settlement of 1916," *Eire-Ireland II* (Autumn, 1967): 132-145. The Easter Rebellion of 1916 led to a readdressing of the Irish question, which had been put on hold by a political truce during war-time. Prime Minister Daniel Lloyd George, on May 11, 1916, announced that he himself would go to Ireland to consult with civil and military authorities about some arrangement for the future.

George. Mary recalls that the prime minister's efforts at achieving an Irish reconciliation failed,[8] and Bill subsequently refused to call his son 'Loyd', preferring to call him 'William'. Loyd's mother and siblings, however, continued to call their newest family member 'Loyd', and the name stuck.

The Ryan's were of hard working country stock and made their living on the family farm, which covered 150 acres on two separate lots of land.[9] While they raised cows and chickens, grew crops and operated a small sugar bush, the bulk of their energies were invested into the rearing of sheep.[10] In the surviving local lore, the Ryan's are remembered as an industrious, hard-working clan. Legend has it that when a barn was being raised in the North Brant

---

[8] Prime Minister George's efforts to investigate the self-governance of the Irish were played out in the "Irish Convention," which first met July 25, 1917 and reported on April 9, 1918, but failed to arrive at an agreement. David W. Savage, "The Parnell of Wales has Become the Chamberlain of England: Lloyd George and the Irish Question," *Journal of British Studies* 12 no. 1 (1972): 86-102.

[9] The Ryan's own one hundred acres across the road from St. Michael's Church and fifty acres where the Ryan homestead was built. Bill and Amelia Ryan originally lived in a little cottage just across from St. Michael's Church, but they moved into Bill's parents' house when they died (Mary Clare, interview with John Perdue, Goderich, ON, November 21, 2009, recording in A).

[10] SOLIA, Mary Clare, letter to John Perdue, January 26, 2012.

region and a wall needed to be lifted, Bill Ryan's voice would cry out "Men of the North, up we go!"[11]

The life of the Ryan family centered around St. Michael's Church.[12] They were one of several Irish Catholic families who emigrated to the North Brant area from Ireland in the mid-eighteen hundreds.[13] These families lived and breathed the Catholic faith. The first Mass to be celebrated in North Brant was celebrated by a missionary priest from Goderich in the home of Loyd's great-grandfather, Edmund Quirk, in 1856.[14] In 1864, under the guidance of Father Hugh Kelly of Riversdale, these pioneer families constructed a log Church on land donated by the Joseph Ferguson family. On this site, guided first by Father Madigan and later by Father Dean Laussie of Walkerton, a new brick structure was erected and opened in 1883.[15] This church functioned as a mission of Sacred Heart Church in Walkerton until the number

---

[11] SOLIA, Mother St. Henry Moloney, SOLI, letter to John Perdue, June 1, 2012, Folder 'A'.

[12] Father Ryan's sister Lucille recalls "It will suffice to say that St. Michael's was the centre of the world…" (St. Michael's Church: North Brant, Ontario 1883-1983. [Hamilton]: 1983, 101).

[13] St. Michael's Church: North Brant, Ontario 1883-1983. [Hamilton]: 1983, 5.

[14] "Golden Jubilee of St. Michael's Parish North Brant, 1883-1933: Held at the Church on Sunday last," *The Walkerton Herald Times*, August 10, 1933. This priest was likely Father Blettner from Goderich (Ibid.).

[15] St. Michael's Church: North Brant, Ontario 1883-1983. [Hamilton]: 1983, 17.

of families it serviced became too small to warrant its continued use and the Church was closed in 1952.[16] Most of St. Michael's Church was destroyed by fire in a tragic act of vandalism on August 21, 1990.[17]

Alongside hard work and contributing to the life of the community, the Catholic faith was an integral component of life in the Ryan household. The Ryan's combined weekly attendance at Sunday Mass with nightly recitation, kneeling around the kitchen table, of the rosary.[18] The walls of the Ryan household were adorned with religious images and spare drawers were filled with Catholic periodicals and holy cards.[19]

---

[16] St. Michael's Church: North Brant, Ontario 1883-1983. [Hamilton]: 1983, 76.

[17] Building Committee of St. Michael's Church, letter to Frank Ryan, June 27, 1991. This letter is in the possession of Mr. Tom Ryan. Now only the façade and the foundation of St. Michael's remains, but Father Ryan's nephew, Paul Ryan, and Hugh Ferguson of North Brant have established the St. Michael's Perpetual Fund, which enables them to maintain the façade and adjoining cemetery for posterity's sake. It is a beautiful testament to the role this Church has played in the shaping of many lives.

[18] Mary Clare, interview by John Perdue, Goderich, ON, November 21, 2009, recording in SOLIA. One might suspect that the Ryan family's devotion to the rosary had been influenced by Father Patrick Peyton's *Family Rosary Crusade*, but this movement was not prevalent in Ontario until the 1940s, at which time Loyd was already a priest (Patrick Peyton, *All for Her; The Autobiography of Father Patrick Peyton, C.S.C.* (Garden City, N.Y.: Doubleday, 1967), 150).

[19] Paul Ryan, interview by John Perdue, North Brant, ON, October 24, 2012, recording in SOLIA.

All of the children received their Sacraments in due course, Loyd being confirmed at St. Anne's Church in Chesley on June 12, 1929 by the Most Rev. John T. McNally, bishop of Hamilton,[20] taking the name John.[21] Loyd's sister, Lucille, remembers as a small child at Mass being aware that "'Holy God we Praise Thy Name' was being sung from the heart of my father and mother."[22] There can be no doubt that the warm, faith-filled environment in which Loyd was raised nourished his nascent vocation. Later in life, when speaking about vocations, Father Loyd would unfailingly stress the importance of strong Catholic family life when it came to inspiring young men to become priests and young women to become religious sisters – he was personally aware of the value of a faith-filled family environment.[23]

Young Loyd's vocation was further nourished by the good example and instruction he received from

---

[20] Diocese of Hamilton Archives (henceforth DHA), Father W.L. Ryan personnel file, Baptismal and Confirmation Record - copy from St. Augustine's Seminary, Toronto, September 6, 1937.

[21] St. Augustine's Seminary Archives (henceforth SASA), Reverend J.C. Leavey of St. Ann's Church, Chesley, ON, letter to St. Augustine's Seminary, May 16, 1937. Father Ryan obtained this notification in order to gain admittance to the seminary.

[22] St. Michael's Church: North Brant, Ontario 1883-1983. [Hamilton]: 1983, 101.

[23] E.g. Father Loyd Ryan, homily preached on Vocations Sunday, May 6, 1990 at St. Clement's Church in St. Clements, ON, SOLIA, Father Ryan homilies, Binder 25.

his childhood pastor, Father John Gilbert Dehler.[24] Father Dehler is lovingly remembered as an energetic priest who tirelessly sought ways to engage the children with the mysteries of their faith.[25] As a small child, Father Ryan's sister Lucille recalls having an awareness that "Fr. Dehler was the emissary of God, given the power through him to change bread and wine into the body and blood of Christ" – sentiments that were no doubt shared by young Loyd Ryan. She also remembers "the catechism sessions with Fr. Dehler during Mass…emphasizing the importance of religion in our lives." The sentiments of the Ryan family toward Father Dehler are summarized in Lucille's referring to him as "our revered Fr. Dehler."[26]

The children's connection to Father Dehler extended beyond attendance at Sunday Mass, too. He encouraged the children of the parish to participate in whatever ministries they could. Mrs. Betty Walker, a former teacher at the parish school, remembers "Father was anxious to have a choir and asked that the children learn the Mass of the Angels in Latin…Most of the children were in the choir, including a brilliant,

---

[24] Father Dehler lived at the pastorate in Chesley from 1926 to 1937. He was succeeded by Father J.C. Leavey, who tended to the pastorate from 1937 to 1941 (St. Michael's Church: North Brant, Ontario 1883-1983. [Hamilton]: 1983, 71).

[25] St. Michael's Church: North Brant, Ontario 1883-1983. [Hamilton]: 1983, 21.

[26] Ibid., 101.

young soloist, Lloyd Ryan, now Father Lloyd Ryan.
Fr. Dehler was very proud of his young choir, as was
I." [27] Father Dehler invited the kids to put on a
Christmas concert at the parish hall in Chesley and
rewarded their efforts with small gifts. [28] Mary
Fleming recalls that "on another occasion Fr. Dehler
treated us to what seemed to be dozens of bricks of ice
cream, rushing out from Chesley with it just in time
for lunch lest it melt."[29] Interestingly, this image of a
kind, fatherly parish priest providing treats to the little
ones is exactly how Father Ryan is himself
remembered by his nieces and nephews.[30] Fr. Dehler
undoubtedly played a role in shaping Father Ryan's
image of the priesthood and in kindling his desire to
pursue his vocation. Observing Father Dehler taught
Loyd a great deal about the priesthood, and
specifically about how a pastor ought to relate to the
children in his parish.

There is one final positive influence that
nourished Loyd's blossoming vocation and shaped his
awareness of what was most important in the work of
fostering faith: the influence of Catholic educators.
Father P.J. Maloney had been appointed to Sacred
Heart Church in Walkerton in 1921, at which time

---

[27] St. Michael's Church: North Brant, Ontario 1883-1983.
[Hamilton]: 1983, 101, 70.
[28] Ibid., 66.
[29] Ibid.
[30] Paul Ryan, interview by John Perdue, North Brant, ON,
October 24, 2012, recording in SOLIA.

there were ten families in North Brant with young children.[31] Father Maloney was a great promoter of Catholic education, and considered these families to be a firm enough foundation on which to establish a small separate school. A portion of St. Michael's Church was partitioned off, and classes began at Separate School Number Eleven in January 1922.[32] His trips to S.S. No. 11 would be the first of Loyd's independent ventures into the wide world, and it is significant that his first forays led him to Catholic school in a Catholic Church. Loyd is remembered as a shy young man,[33] and it was important that his inaugural encounter with society should be a positive one. This it was, and his pleasant experience of the separate school system made a deep impression on him.

Loyd's schooling began with Miss Eleanor Kennedy, his first teacher. Miss Kennedy's profound faith is evidenced by the fact that just two and a half years after assuming her teaching position, she would leave North Brant to join the Sisters of St. Joseph in Hamilton, where she became Sister Patrice.[34] Miss Kennedy was replaced by Miss Margaret McCurdy,

---

[31] St. Michael's Church: North Brant, Ontario 1883-1983. [Hamilton]: 1983, 63.
[32] Ibid.
[33] Mary Clare, interview with John Perdue, Goderich, ON, November 21, 2009, recording in SOLIA.
[34] St. Michael's Church: North Brant, Ontario 1883-1983. [Hamilton]: 1983, 64.

16

who was in turn replaced by Miss Betty Tully.[35] It was she who, under the direction of Father Dehler, taught the students the settings for the Missa De Angelis, as well as the Benediction hymns and the *Stabat Mater*. Instruction in the faith was an integral component of education at S.S. No. 11, where the teachers played a significant role in preparing the students for their sacraments and taught them many prayers.[36]

Young Loyd "sailed through" his elementary years, skipping grades at times.[37] Kathleen O'Reilly attended S.S. No. 11 with him, and she recalls being unexpectedly made aware that "the teacher had fitted Loyd in an advanced class."[38] Due to his rapid advancement, Loyd passed his high school entrance examination in 1928, just three weeks after his eleventh birthday. Two years previously, S.S. No. 11, which had begun by offering only elementary grades, had expanded to offer grades nine and ten, called "continuation school" at the time.[39] Tax support for

---

[35] Miss Tully's married name was Betty Walker.

[36] St. Michael's Church: North Brant, Ontario 1883-1983. [Hamilton]: 1983, 64.

[37] Mary Clare, interview with John Perdue, Goderich, ON, November 21, 2009, recording in SOLIA.

[38] SOLIA, Kathleen O'Reilly, letter to John Perdue, July 9, 2003, folder 'A'.

[39] St. Michael's Church: North Brant, Ontario 1883-1983. [Hamilton]: 1983, 65. For a history of the expansion of the Separate School System in Ontario, see Michael Power, *A Promise Fulfilled: Highlights in the Political History of Catholic Separate Schools in Ontario* (Toronto: Ontario Catholic School Trustees' Association, 2002).

separate schools in Ontario during these years was much lower than that for public schools and would not support a complete Catholic secondary education.[40] The insufficient funding of Catholic schools placed particular pressure on rural Catholic schools like S.S. No. 11, where a change in the system of rural school grants had already made budgets very slim.[41] The addition of continuation classes at country schools like S.S. No. 11 placed a heavy burden on teachers, who were asked to accommodate older students.[42] This burden was borne admirably by the educators at S.S. No. 11, where Loyd was able to finish grade ten in June 1930.

Looking back, it is almost as if Loyd's elementary school had been established specifically with him in mind – as a result of having completed ten years of education in just eight years he is perhaps the only student to have graduated every grade offered at S.S. No. 11.[43] Miss Monica Flanigan from Guelph was the last teacher at the school, which closed due to declining enrollment in 1930, after just eight years of

---

[40] Franklin A. Walker, *Catholic Education and Politics in Ontario Volume II* (Toronto: The Federation of Catholic Education Associations of Ontario, 1974), 322.

[41] Ibid., 327.

[42] St. Michael's Church: North Brant, Ontario 1883-1983. [Hamilton]: 1983, 65.

[43] Father Ryan's elder brothers Dan and Frank were among the first pupils at S.S. No. 11, but Father himself was only four years old when the school opened, and would not attend until September, 1922 (St. Michael's Church: North Brant, Ontario 1883-1983. [Hamilton]: 1983, 63).

operation. Father Ryan deeply treasured his Catholic education, and it became a hallmark of his priesthood to strive with every fibre of his being to see to it that others were afforded the same opportunity to come to know Jesus that he had received.

An amendment to the Adolescent Attendance Schools Act in 1921 made it necessary for all children in Ontario to attend school until the age of sixteen.[44] In the absence of a fully funded system of Catholic secondary education,, Catholic families like the Ryan's were obliged to send their children to public school to finish their high school education. In Loyd's case, he was awarded a scholarship to Upper Canada College (UCC) in Toronto in 1930. The family declined the award, however, largely because Loyd had his heart and mind set on the Holy Priesthood and not the professional career that a UCC education would prepare him for.[45] His sister Mary Clare cannot remember Loyd ever having considered another vocation.[46] Loyd's mother, too, was hesitant to part ways with her son, which may have factored into the decision to decline the scholarship to UCC. Thus it was that Loyd completed the final three years of his high school education at nearby Chesley High. No record of his performance during the final years of

---

[44] Power, 250.

[45] SOLIA, Mary Fleming, letter to SOLI community, undated [likely 2003].

[46] Mary Clare, interview with John Perdue, Goderich, ON, November 21, 2009, recording in SOLIA.

high school exists today, but Loyd's sister Mary
remembers that he continued to demonstrate a high
aptitude for studies and that he was involved in
"everything," including football, hockey and
baseball.[47]

Seminary Days

Upon completion of his high school studies,
Loyd Ryan applied to the philosophy program at St.
Jerome's College in Waterloo, where he was
accepted, lived and studied from 1932 to 1935. In the
Hamilton diocese at that time, the philosophy
component of a young man's formation for the
priesthood – also referred to as the "arts" program –
was commonly completed at St. Jerome's college. The
college had been founded in 1865 by Father Louis
Funcken, C.R., and continues to be overseen by the
Congregation of the Resurrection. The founding
mission of St. Jerome's was the education of young
men for the priesthood and other professional
careers.[48] Loyd went through St. Jerome's during the
very tumultuous depression era, when the future of the

---

[47] Mary Clare, interview with John Perdue, Goderich, ON,
November 21, 2009, recording in SOLIA.

[48] Kenneth McLaughlin, Gerald Stortz and James Wahl,
*Enthusiasm for the Truth: An Illustrated History of St.
Jerome's University* (Waterloo: St. Jerome's University,
2002), 37.

college was uncertain and while Father Robert Dehler, C.R., served as president.[49]

Times were tough and the accommodations at St. Jerome's were not altogether comfortable in the early 1930s, but, as he had done in earlier years, Loyd excelled in his studies and gave himself fully to the formation program. Records indicate that he was an "outstanding member of the St. Jerome's College track and field team" and a promoter in the League of the Sacred Heart from 1934-35.[50] He graduated on June 6, 1935 with a diploma from the philosophy department, having won the Kraehn Medal for General History.[51] In a letter from the vice president of St. Jerome's, Father William G. Borho, C.R., to the rector of St. Augustine's, dated September 9, 1936, Father Borho says "He was a student somewhat above the average, is of good character, was consistent in the observance of the rules of the institution, and in the practice of piety. Altogether, he has shown in his conduct all that could be desired of a student preparing himself for the priesthood. We gladly recommend him as one deserving of consideration."[52]

A small firestorm seems to have broken out when Loyd completed his philosophy studies and set

---

[49] McLaughlin et al., 120.
[50] SOLIA, Father James Wahl, C.R., email to John Perdue, October 15, 2012.
[51] Ibid.
[52] SASA, Father William G. Borho, C.R., letter to the rector of St. Augustine's Seminary, September 9, 1936.

his eyes toward the major seminary. Most likely through exposure to their publications, he had become enamoured of the Missionary Oblates of Mary Immaculate (OMI), an attachment that created quite a stir.[53] Loyd wrote a letter in 1935, at eighteen years of age, asking the Right Reverend J. McNally, bishop of the iocese of Hamilton, to send a testimonial letter to Rev. Michael Murphy, OMI, the novice master of the Holy Rosary Novitiate of the Oblates in Ottawa. This letter, however, was never sent.[54] It turns out that Ryan's mother was adamantly opposed to her son becoming a missionary. Loyd's sister, Mary, remembers her mother weeping over the thought of her son ministering far away from home, in the cold north.[55]

One can imagine that a considerable debate was held in the Ryan household before a revised letter

---

[53] Oblate publications, including one from their Canadian National Missionary Exhibition in Toronto in 1940, were found at the Ryan family farm in North Brant.

[54] This letter is in the possession of Mr. Paul Ryan, Father Ryan's nephew. There is no evidence of the letter in the Hamilton Diocesan archives. The archives of the OMIs contain no correspondence from Loyd Ryan (SOLIA, Father André Duboi, email to John Perdue, January 25, 2013).

[55] Mary Clare, interview with John Perdue, Goderich, ON, November 21, 2009, recording in SOLIA. Paul Ryan likewise confirms that Father Loyd's mother did not want him to become a missionary priest (Paul Ryan, interview by John Perdue, North Brant, ON, March 27, 2012, recording in SOLIA).

was finally sent to Bishop McNally. The normal course of events for a young man discerning a call to the priesthood is to approach his bishop and request admission to the seminary. In his letter, written in August 1935, Loyd asked Bishop McNally to undertake a course of study for the diocesan priesthood in his diocese. It seems that young Mr. Ryan had received inside information that St. Augustine's Seminary in Toronto had a very high number of applicants, because he indicated to the Bishop that if there was no room for him in the seminary, he would appreciate the bishop sending a testimonial letter to the Novice Master of the Oblate's Holy Rosary Novitiate. A trace of Irish stubbornness can be seen in this letter laden with compromise. Loyd was issued an answer on August 31, 1935, indicating that there was no room in the seminary, and that the bishop could write a testimonial letter if he were to receive letters from Loyd's pastor and from the Father Superior of the OMIs.[56]

There is no evidence of Loyd having obtained the necessary letters of recommendation from his pastor nor from the Father Superior of the OMIs. The family decided to wait for a year before Loyd would reapply for admission to the diocesan seminary. This decision was not an easy one, and Loyd likely suffered very much in having to postpone his

---

[56] DHA, Father W.L. Ryan personnel file, letter from Bishop J. McNally to Loyd Ryan, August 31, 1935.

formation, since his desire to become a priest was very strong. It was decided that he would stay at home and work on the family farm for a year. His sister recalls that her mother was very upset "to think that she may have spoiled his vocation."[57]

When the allotted time had passed, Loyd reapplied for admission to studies for the diocese of Hamilton and was accepted at St. Augustine's Seminary in Scarborough, Ontario. His letter of acceptance to the seminary is dated Aug. 31, 1936,[58] and his sister Mary Clare remembers her mother's great delight at the news.[59] Indeed, his mother's over-attentiveness to Loyd's vocation at times drew attention. Completing the mandatory pastoral reference for seminary admission, Loyd's pastor, J.C. Leavey, in response to the question 'what is the public opinion about his vocation?' wrote "at times questioned. Some have expressed themselves by saying there might be a bit of parental influence" and "the over-solicitude of the parents to have a son a priest might have a mild influence on Mr. Ryan."[60]

---

[57] Mary Clare, interview by John Perdue, Goderich, ON, November 21, 2009, recording in SOLIA.

[58] SASA, Father William G. Borho, C.R., letter to the rector of St. Augustine's Seminary, September 9, 1936. A copy of this letter can be found in SOLIA.

[59] Mary Clare, interview by John Perdue, Goderich, ON, November 21, 2009, recording in SOLIA.

[60] SASA, J.C. Leavy, "Investigation to be Made by Pastors Before Seminarians are Promoted to Ordination," September 12, 1937. This investigation was completed prior to Ryan's admittance to minor orders.

Ryan's 60 years of priesthood leave little room for doubt about the authenticity of his vocation, but one cannot help wondering what influence his mother's somewhat overbearing personality had upon him. Ryan was undoubtedly a strong-willed priest - a determination that served him well in many respects - but some parishioners considered him to be imperious in his mannerisms, a trait he may well have picked up from his mother.[61]

Loyd began his theology studies at St. Augustine's Seminary on September 14, 1936.[62] At that time, Monsignor Edward Michael Brennan was rector, Father William T. Davis was vice-rector and Father John Henry Ingoldsby was prefect of discipline.[63] During Loyd's time, all theology courses were offered within the seminary building, where the foci were dogmatic and moral theology, sacred scripture and canon law. Also covered were ascetical theology (the spiritual life), pastoral theology and ecclesiastical history.[64] The spiritual formation of

---

[61] Nancy Parks, telephone interview by John Perdue, June 2, 2012, transcript in SOLIA.

[62] SASA, Monsignor E.M. Brennan, president of St. Augustine's Seminary, letter to Loyd Ryan, August 31, 1936.

[63] Richard J. Dobell, *Fifty Golden Years: St. Augustine's Seminary, Toronto Ontario* (Toronto: Mission Press, 1963), 32.

[64] Booth, Karen Marshall, ed. *The People Cry – 'Send us Priests': The First Seventy-five Years of St. Augustine's Seminary of Toronto, 1913-1988 Part I* (Toronto: Metro Press, 1988), 12.

seminarians included regular spiritual direction, nightly spiritual conferences, and such daily devotions as the rosary, morning and night prayer, visits to the Blessed Sacrament and general examinations of conscience.[65] Before the noon and evening meals the seminarians took turns reading short spiritual reflections from a pulpit in the refectory.

During Loyd's formational years, St. Augustine's Seminary had a reputation for sternness and discipline. Conformity to the daily horarium (schedule) and to the faculty's expectations for conduct were strictly enforced. Seminarians rose at 5:30 to busy days of study, spiritual exercises and structured recreation periods, ending each evening with the rosary, night prayer and an examination of conscience before lights out at 9:45 pm. Permission to leave the seminary grounds was only granted for fifteen days during the Christmas season and for summer holidays.[66] Seminarians were not permitted to study in groups unless express permission had been given and they were not permitted to have food, radio, magazines or newspapers in their rooms. While Loyd certainly learned discipline during his time at seminary, his natural orderliness and affinity for structure likely contributed to his success at St. Augustine's, where he sailed through without incident, receiving each of the minor orders in due

---

[65] Booth, 13.
[66] Ibid., 15.

course.[67] There can be little doubt that the regimented formation that Loyd received shaped his approach to ministry and to the spiritual life. Later in life, he developed a reputation for punctuality and orderliness both in his ministry and in his personal life.[68] That Loyd enjoyed his time at St. Augustine's is evident from the fondness with which he would reminisce about his seminary days, often referring to St. Augustine's as his 'alma mater'.[69]

When the time came for Loyd to be ordained he was just 23 years of age. Because, at that time, canon law stipulated a minimum age of 24 for admission to major orders, a dispensation had to be obtained from Rome before he could be ordained.[70]

---

[67] Father Ryan's seminary journal (SOLIA) records the most significant dates in his seminary journey:
Entered Seminary - Mon, Sept. 14th, 1936
Received First Tonsure - Wed. June 8th, 1938
First Minors - Thurs. June 9th 1938
Second Minors - Sat. Sept. 24th 1938
Subdeaconate - Sat. June 3rd 1939
Deaconate - Sat. Sept. 23rd, 1939
Priesthood - Sunday, June 9th, 1940
[68] Patricia White and Janet Pfaffinger, interview by John Perdue, St. Clements, ON, December 28, 2011, recording in SOLIA.
[69] Mother St. Henry Moloney, SOLI, interview by John Perdue, Cambridge, ON, November 20, 2009, recording in SOLIA.
[70] Catholic Church. *Codex iuris canonici Pii X Pontificis Maximi iussu digestus, Benedicti Papae XV auctoritate promulgatus* (Romae: Typis Polyglottis Vaticanis, 1917), Canon 975.

This dispensation was obtained[71] and Loyd Ryan was ordained a priest by Bishop Joseph F. Ryan at the Cathedral of Christ the King in Hamilton on June 9, 1940.[72] To the delight of family and friends, Father Loyd celebrated his first Solemn High Mass at St. Michael's in North Brant on Sunday, June 16, 1940.[73] This would be the first of many Masses offered by Father Ryan at his home parish. Later, with the permission of Bishop Ryan, Father Loyd continued to celebrate an annual Mass at St. Michael's even after the church's closure.[74]

Priestly Ministry

Ryan's formation, though, did not end when his seminary days drew to a close. A strong priestly identity must be fashioned by means of a long and

---

[71] Paul Ryan, interview by John Perdue, North Brant, ON, October 24, 2012, recording in SOLIA.

[72] "Four Receive Holy Orders: Bishop Will Ordain At Cathedral in Hamilton," *The Catholic Standard*, June 1940, Vol. 1 No. 7.

[73] "Ordination on Sunday Next: Father Lloyd Ryan of North Brant Will Celebrate First Mass in Home Parish on Sunday, the 16th of June," *The Chesley Enterprise*, June 6, 1940.

[74] This happened on the first Sunday of August and attracted many of the current and former residents of North Brant. Mass was followed by a folk music concert, a picnic, games for the children and oftentimes a bonfire in the evening for those who stayed the whole day.

committed life of service. In Father Ryan's case, he learned what it meant to be a priest in the context of a robust pastoral ministry. He served in many parishes, rural and urban, large and small, throughout his 63 years of priestly ministry in the diocese of Hamilton.[75] Besides that of 'pastor', Ryan was obliged to wear many other hats during these years. He served on the Diocesan Council for a number of years, beginning in 1962 when he was pastor at Sacred Heart Church in Mildmay.[76] Also during his pastorate at Sacred Heart, Ryan served on the Diocesan Vocation Committee, having been appointed by Bishop Reding in 1963.[77] While he was stationed at the flagship parish of Church of Our Lady in Guelph from 1969 to 1979, Ryan served as Dean of the Wellington County Deanery.[78] And throughout the duration of his ministry, he served as chaplain to numerous lay associations at both the parochial and diocesan levels.

In every ministry he undertook and in each appointment he was given, Ryan was aware that he was called to put his life at the service of the faithful.

---

[75] For a list of parishes in which Father Ryan served, see Appendix B.

[76] DHA, Bishop Ryan file, letter from Bishop Ryan to Father Ryan, May 31, 1962.

[77] Father Ryan wrote "I will be happy to do anything I can re: vocations" (DHA, Mildmay-Sacred Heart file P93, letter from Father Ryan to V. Rev. Paul F. Reding, December 2, 1963).

[78] DHA, Bishop Reding file, letter from Bishop Reding to Father Ryan, June 19, 1979.

An ordained minister exercises this duty of service to the people of God by teaching, governing and sanctifying.[79] Ryan's faithfulness to his vocation can be understood by observing his active pastoral ministry through the lens of this three-fold office.[80] From this perspective, a picture of Ryan's pastoral ministry can be constructed. This picture will help to understand what young men or women considering a religious vocation may have been attracted to in Father Ryan.

In terms of his teaching office, the primary means through which Ryan instructed his parishioners was the Sunday homily. He carefully prepared and handwrote every sermon he ever delivered, and virtually all of them are extant today.[81] He kept them in chronologically ordered binders and referred back to them regularly, often re-working something he had said in a previous year for use in a new context. He preached from the notes he had prepared, and his presentation style was not particularly dynamic.[82] Still, homilies delivered by Ryan have been described as "substantial" and "brave". When the readings

---

[79] *Catechism of the Catholic Church*, article 1592.

[80] While it proved very difficult to succinctly and coherently present 52 years of active priestly ministry, this three-fold structure presented itself as a plausible way forward.

[81] These homilies are kept in the Sisters of Our Lady Immaculate Archives.

[82] Gerry Doucette, interview by John Perdue, Cambridge, ON, December 29, 2011, recording in SOLIA.

addressed sensitive subject matter, Ryan did not skirt the issue, but "went right after it."[83]

Ryan was very well read, a characteristic that came through in his homilies and talks, where he frequently made reference to a periodical or book he had been reading.[84] His reading selections tended to be drawn from traditional, neo-scholastic authors and from the writings or biographies of the saints. That he was convincing and winsome in his presentation of the faith is evident from the number of non-Catholic Christians who attended Mass with their spouses and would approach Father Ryan to express their desire to enter the faith.[85] It was often observed that those who had been converted to the Catholic faith through the example and instruction of Father Ryan were among the most devout and zealous parishioners.

---

[83] Gerry Doucette, interview by John Perdue, Cambridge, ON, December 29, 2011, recording in SOLIA.

[84] Examples of books and periodicals referred to in Father Ryan's homilies; *Messenger*, a publication of the Institute of Religious Studies, December 1987/January 1988, Vol IV, No. 4-5 (SOLIA, Father Ryan's homilies, Binder 17), Publications from The Marian Movement of Priests (July 3, 1987, Binder 17), periodical *Sursum Corda* (Aug. 3, 1997, Binder 30), The Marian News (June 26, 1994, Binder 28), The Imitation of Christ (Binder 23), Father Le Buffe's *Visits* (June 6, 1993, Binder 27), Columbia Magazine (Binder 27), Lay Witness, the EWTN Family Newsletter, and the Coalition in Support of Ecclesia Dei.

[85] SOLIA, Catharine Collins, email to John Perdue, March 21, 2011.

Ryan brought a warm and inviting demeanor to his role as shepherd of the faithful. His kindliness made him very easy to approach.[86] When he was pastor at St. John's in Dundalk from 1958 to 1960, he would visit the Osprey Mission, where several families would come for Mass. Sister Kathleen Haley (SSND) recalls how well loved Father Ryan was among this intimate group, and how he took special interest in the development of the youngest family members. Her brother Frank credits Father Ryan with opening his social and spiritual horizons by introducing him to the CYO movement, which had a large, multi-parish presence in the Hamilton diocese at the time.[87] It was characteristic of Ryan to care not only for the spiritual wellbeing of his parishioners, but also to their physical and social needs as well. He never hesitated, for example, to invite couples and families for meals at his rectory, especially where poverty was a concern.[88]

Everywhere he was assigned, Father Ryan promoted or established parish groups and activities

---

[86] SOLIA, Sister Joan McMahon, CSJ, letter to SOLI Sisters, February 6, 2013, Folder 'B'. Sister Joan remembers Father Ryan when he was associate pastor at St. Mary's in Brantford, where the schoolchildren "found Father Ryan very approachable."

[87] SOLIA, Sister Kathleen Haley, SSND, email to John Perdue, February 13, 2012.

[88] SOLIA, Catharine Collins, email to John Perdue, March 21, 2011.

and established life-long relationships.[89] He started a boxing club for boys at Sacred Heart Church in Guelph in 1943,[90] organized hockey games during the winter months at the Church or Our Lady in Guelph in the 1970s,[91] recruited parishioners – even those of German descent - to celebrate St. Patrick's Day at St. Clement's in St. Clements in the 1980s, [92] and everywhere found time for parish groups like the Blue Army, the Youth Club, the Christian Mother's Society, and senior citizens' clubs.[93]

In his role as leader, Father Ryan adhered faithfully to the Magisterium of the Church, and at times this caused him great pain. While he was stationed at St. Clement's Church, he caught wind of a

---

[89] Mr. Tom Ryan is in possession of a letter from Father Ryan to his brother Frank, dated simply '1993,' wherein Father Ryan writes "I am expecting 3 lads from Brantford on Monday. They were members of the C.Y.O. when I was there 40 years ago. So they will have changed quite a bit. It's nice to see people whom you haven't seen in a long time." Father Loyd Ryan, letter to Frank Ryan, 1993.

[90] Mother St. Henry Moloney, SOLI, interview by John Perdue, Cambridge, ON, December 29, 2011, recording in SOLIA.

[91] SOLIA, Mike Manera, e-mail to John Perdue, May 8, 2011.

[92] Patricia White and Janet Pfaffinger, interview by John Perdue, St. Clements, ON, December 28, 2011, recording in SOLIA.

[93] Janet Pfaffinger and Patricia White, *St. Clement's Roman Catholic Parish 160 Years: 1847-2007 and St. Clement's Roman Catholic Church 150 Years: 1858-2008* (St. Jacobs: St. Jacobs Printery, 2008), 31.

rumour that he was denying some parishioners the Sacraments, especially marriage. This accusation arose as a result of Father's expressed desire that both husband and wife should be Catholic and, if either party were not, that they should undergo instruction and receive baptism and/or confirmation. If, however, circumstances made this untenable, Father Ryan did not refuse to preside over any marriage. In fact, records from St. Clement's Church indicate that approximately one third of the marriages over which he presided involved a Catholic and a non-Catholic party, making the accusations leveled against him unfair. In an undated response found amongst his possessions, Ryan wrote "If the purpose of this was to hurt the priest – you have succeeded – It is entirely false. I learned early in my priesthood to do all I could to help people and if the laws of God & the Church allowed it at all, to bend over backwards to permit people to receive the Grace of the Sacraments."

Ryan was not afraid to give public witness to his principles, if the care of his parishioners demanded it. While he was pastor at Church of Our Lady in Guelph in the 1970s, the *Catholic Register* – to Ryan's dismay – published several articles that demonstrated questionable theology. The straw that broke the camel's back was an article in Father Joseph Killoran's weekly column *One Pastor's Thoughts*. On September 22 1973, in an article entitled *Humanae Vitae – 5 Years Later*, Father Killoran argued that the ongoing confusion among moral theologians and among the Catholic faithful on the issue of birth control left the Church's teaching on the subject "very much in doubt." He concluded his article thus: "As far then, as birth control is concerned, it seems to me that for the time being at least Catholics may use artificial contraception in perfectly good faith."[94] Father Ryan, upon reading this article, felt that he could no longer make the *Register* available to his parishioners in good conscience. He notified Bishop Reding of his intention to cancel the parish subscription and Bishop Reding responded that Father Ryan was "quite justified" in doing so.[95] He wrote a strong letter to then-editor Mr. Shaun MacGrath on September 25, 1973. He did this because, as he explained, "when this Catholic paper sees fit to print articles that can seriously harm the people for whom I have a responsibility before God, I can no longer in conscience make the paper available to them through our parish channels."[96]

In 1990, when Father Ryan was pastor at St. Clement's Church in St. Clements and nearing his retirement, Brian Mulroney's Progressive Conservative federal government introduced Bill C-43, which would render doctors susceptible to jail

---

[94] Joseph M. Killoran, "Humanae Vitae – 5 Years Later," *The Catholic Register*, September 22, 1973.

[95] DHA, letter from Bishop Reding to Father Loyd Ryan, Sept. 28, 1973 file P36-007-006.

[96] DHA, letter from Father Ryan to Mr. Shaun MacGrath, publisher and general manager, Catholic Register Sept. 25, 1973 file P36-007-006.

time for denying abortions in cases where the mother's health was at risk.[97] Father Ryan wrote several letters to municipal, provincial and federal parliamentarians urging them to vote down Bill C-43,[98] and he regularly encouraged his parishioners to do the same. Bill C-43 passed the House of Commons but died in the Senate.

While he provided guidance and leadership in secular matters, Ryan knew that his first duty was to tend to the sanctification of his people. The first and foremost means through which he endeavoured to fulfill this mission was through the administration of the Sacraments. The Second Vatican Council taught that the Eucharist is the source and summit of the Christian life,[99] and Ryan celebrated it with focus and reverence, conveying his deep respect for the sacred mysteries through careful gestures and movements.[100]

---

[97] "Abortion Rights: Significant Moments in Canadian History," CBC News, accessed July 31, 2013, http://www.cbc.ca/news/canada/story/2009/01/13/f-abortion-timeline.html.

[98] E.g. SOLIA, Father Loyd Ryan, letter to Bob Rae re: abortion, February 21, 1991, Father Ryan homilies, Binder 25; Father Loyd Ryan, letter to Dr. Harry Brightwell, M.P. re: Bill C-43 (abortion), January 22, 1990, carbon copied to the Right Honourable Brian Mulroney, Prime Minister, and to the Honourable Doug Lewis, Minister of Justice, Father Ryan homilies, Binder 25.

[99] Pope Paul VI, *Lumen Gentium* (Light of the Nations), November 21, 1964, www.vatican.va, 11.

[100] Father Patric D'Arcy, telephone interview by John Perdue, Scarborough, ON, October 26, 2012, recording in SOLIA.

He would genuflect slowly, enunciate the words of the Mass attentively and handle and purify the sacred vessels reverently. Parishioners noted his respect for the Mass and were encouraged to adopt a similar disposition.[101] Ryan is also remembered as a gifted and gentle confessor[102] whose advice was simple, straightforward and practical.[103] This was undoubtedly the product of the careful preparations he made for hearing confessions – among his possessions was found an entire binder of small notes he had written by hand and entitled "Confessional Notes for the Confessor."[104] This binder contained spiritual nuggets meant for use in the confessional.

Though always busy as a pastor, Ryan also found time to offer spiritual direction when he could, and is remembered for his kindness and his helpfulness.[105] He culled insights from his own spiritual life in his efforts to encourage others in their

---

[101] SOLIA, Doris Azzopardi, memories of Father Ryan, October 22, 2003. Doris served as Father's housekeeper at St. Clement's Church in St. Clements from 1979 to 1982.
[102] Herb Altmann, interview by John Perdue, Kitchener, ON, December 29, 2011, recording in SOLIA.
[103] SOLIA, Sister Mary Catherine Perdue, SOLI, memories of Father Ryan, August 2003; Father Patric D'Arcy, telephone interview by John Perdue, Scarborough, ON October 26, 2012, recording in SOLIA.
[104] SOLIA, Father Ryan's homilies, Binder 14.
[105] SOLIA, Sister Mary Catherine Perdue, SOLI, memories of Father Ryan, August 2003; Father Patric D'Arcy, telephone interview by John Perdue, Scarborough, ON October 26, 2012, recording in SOLIA.

walk with the Lord. The pillars of his personal spiritual life were the Mass and devotion to Our Lord in the Blessed Sacrament,[106] a deep life of prayer,[107] devotion to the Blessed Virgin Mary and the saints, and a commitment to many other devotions that fostered a pious interior disposition.

His personal spiritual life spilled over into Ryan's ministry as well, where his parishioners were encouraged by his example and his advice. For his fourth assignment, he was appointed associate pastor at St. Mary's in Brantford from 1947 to 1958. There, it is recalled that his prayer life evinced deep devotion to the Blessed Sacrament and won the respect and admiration of his parishioners. [108] The same prayerfulness was noted much later in Ryan's ministry, when he was pastor at St. Clement's Church in St. Clements from 1979 to 1992. Patricia White served as Father Ryan's secretary during these years, where the parishioners remember him constantly praying in the Church before the Blessed Sacrament. Whenever a cheque needed to be signed and Father Loyd could not be found, Patricia would go to the Church and find him on his knees before the

---

[106] Patricia White and Janet Pfaffinger, interview by John Perdue, St. Clements, ON, December 28, 2011, recording in SOLIA.
[107] See Appendix C.
[108] SOLIA, Catharine Collins, email to John Perdue, March 21, 2011.

tabernacle.[109] Father would rise, sign the cheque, and be back on his knees before she had left the Church.[110]

In his efforts to foster devotion in the hearts of his parishioners, Ryan encouraged many pious organizations and devotions. He was spiritual director to the Legion of Mary in his parishes, and he routinely organized events like the Block Rosary, the May procession and crowning of Mary and pilgrimages to Marian Shrines. His Corpus Christi processions were magnificent, and even drew in parishioners from neighbouring parishes.[111] He saw value in any external sign, habit or devotion that fostered the life of grace. He consequently encouraged his parishioners in their own devotions; to participate in St. Louis Marie de Montfort's total consecration to the Blessed Virgin Mary; to fill their homes with prayer cards or relics; and to read and speak constantly about the saints, whom Ryan loved deeply and desired to see honoured and emulated.[112]

The top of every page Ryan wrote was inscribed 'JMJ' (Jesus, Mary and Joseph), and he jotted 'St. A.G.' (Saint Anne's Guidance) at the

---

[109] Patricia White and Janet Pfaffinger, interview by John Perdue, St. Clements, ON, December 28, 2011, recording in SOLIA.

[110] Ibid.

[111] Ibid.

[112] Herb Altmann, interview by John Perdue, St. Clements, ON, December 29, 2011, recording in SOLIA.

bottom left corner of every letter he mailed.[113] He also blessed himself or tipped his hat whenever he passed a Catholic Church or a cemetery.[114] Ryan was most passionate in keeping Lent by fasting and Lenten devotions like the stations of the cross, showing a good example to his parishioners.[115] He ate only bread and drank only water on Fridays, and wore his cassock regularly and his biretta at times because he felt that a priest ought to be identifiable for the people.[116] All of these small external devotions were means by which Ryan nurtured his own spiritual life and that of his parishioners.

There is ample evidence, too, of Ryan's faithfulness to his duties of teaching, governance and sanctification. His fidelity to his ministry can be seen, for example, in the love shown him by his parishioners. The most noteworthy manifestation of this love and appreciation came at the conclusion of Father Ryan's term as associate pastor at St. Mary's in Brantford. He was so well loved at this parish that when he left in 1958 the community bought him a

---

[113] E.g. Father Loyd Ryan, letter to Frank Ryan, August 3, 1994. This letter is in the possession of Mr. Tom Ryan.
[114] SOLIA, Michael Manera, email to John Perdue, May 8, 2011.
[115] SOLIA, Rita Runstedler, letter to John Perdue, January 7, 2012.
[116] Patricia White and Janet Pfaffinger, interview by John Perdue, St. Clements, ON, December 28, 2011, recording in SOLIA.

car.[117] Until that point he had not owned a vehicle and had travelled about the parish by bicycle. The warmth and love that he received from his parishioners expressed their appreciation for Ryan's constant gift of self in ministry.

In 1979, when Ryan was moved from the Church of Our Lady in Guelph to St. Clement's in St. Clements, Bishop Paul F. Reding wrote "It has been my privilege and pleasure to be associated with you as a brother priest for all of my priesthood and I have ample example of the warmth and affection of a truly pastoral priest."[118] Later, when Father Ryan retired from St. Clement's in 1992, the then-auxiliary bishop of Hamilton, the Most Reverend Matthew F. Ustrzycki, wrote to him "I have held you in high esteem from the day I got to know you as a fellow priest in this Diocese many years ago. You have served the Church of Hamilton well and your love of the Priesthood of Jesus Christ was and is evident in so many ways."[119] Bishop Anthony F. Tonnos observed at that time "The respect and gratitude which are

_____

[117] Pat recalls that Father Ryan would come frequently and visit with her family, and he showed genuine interest in the children and their aspirations. Father Ryan began a local chapter of the Legion of Mary, convincing Pat to join at the age of ten. SOLIA, Pat Martin, letter to SOLI Sisters, August 27, 2003.
[118] DHA, Bishop Reding file, letter from Bishop Reding to Father Ryan, June 19, 1979.
[119] DHA, Father W.L. Ryan personnel file, letter from Bishop Ustrzycki to Father Ryan, June 15, 1992.

shown to you by many people throughout the Diocese are indeed well deserved and in themselves are indicators of your priestly zeal and ministry. I thank you very sincerely for the wonderful dedication which you have always shown to the people during the time that I was Bishop in this Diocese and also for your loyalty to me as Bishop."[120] These accolades reflect the well-deserved reputation that Ryan had won as a beloved pastor and a guardian of souls.

The love that his parishioners showed him and the kind words written of him at his retirement demonstrate Father Ryan's warm, incarnational approach to the priesthood. He understood that he was called to be another Christ – teaching, governing and sanctifying the faithful – and he brought an inviting and joyful disposition to his ministry. There can be no doubt that it was in the ordinary encounters of parish life that young men and women observed Father Ryan's conduct and were inspired to consider giving their lives to God as priests or religious. They saw in his ministry the external manifestation of his firm religious identity, and it was this that attracted them. Their hearts were hungry for the communion with Christ at the root of Ryan's ministry.

---

[120] DHA, Father W.L. Ryan personnel file, letter from Bishop Tonnos to Father Ryan, March 24, 1992.

The Lighter Side of Father Ryan

While we have seen that Ryan could be quite firm when it was necessary, he was generally quite jovial, and reminiscences about him invariably include several amusing anecdotes. Many of these come from nieces and nephews who have very fond memories of time spent on the family farm with Father Ryan, where he engaged their young imaginations with boating, fishing, shooting and swimming.[121] He was the "center of the universe" to them, as one nephew put it.[122] But it was not only to his nieces and nephews that Father Ryan brought joy – he brought it everywhere he went. Parishioners remember his quick smile and Irish wit, oftentimes with his head tilted mischievously.[123] Father went all out on St. Patrick's Day, organizing parish socials with dancing, Irish music, jokes and food. Everyone in the parish became Irish with him – at St. Clements, the typically German parishioners became the O'Hergotts, O'Hinchbergers and O'Dietrichs.[124]

---

[121] Refer to Appendix D for memories of Father Ryan recorded by Father Ryan's nieces and nephews.
[122] SOLIA, Bill Sampson, email to John Perdue, October 12, 2012.
[123] Patricia White and Janet Pfaffinger, interview by John Perdue, St. Clements, ON, December 28, 2011, recording in SOLIA.
[124] SOLIA, Rita Runstedler, letter to John Perdue, January 7, 2012.

Father Ryan is remembered as a keen euchre and bridge player, who would often take risks on his hands, but more often than not pull through.[125] He was an avid hunter and fisherman,[126] hobbies that brought with them many comical adventures.[127] He would often spend his vacations helping make raspberry, cherry or apple preserves at the family farm, or assisting at the 'sugar shack' in maple syrup season.[128] In his later years, when the family farm was in decline, Father Ryan enjoyed long drives through the fields of his youth.[129] Getting even further in touch with his roots, Ryan used the gifts he received at his retirement to take a trip with his siblings to Ireland from Sept. 13 to Sept. 27, 1991, at which time he arranged to have his name placed on the tombstone of the Ryan clan when he died.[130]

---

[125] SOLIA, Marie Ryan, memories recorded and sent by e-mail from Tom Ryan to John Perdue, July 7, 2012.

[126] DHA, letter from Fr. Ryan to Bishop Ryan, November 6, 1961, file P93; DHA, letter from Fr. Ryan to Bishop Reding, October 17, 1980, file P112.

[127] See Appendix E for several stories related to Father Ryan's hunting and fishing adventures.

[128] Father Loyd Ryan, letter to Frank Ryan, March 11, 1982. This letter is in the possession of Mr. Tom Ryan.

[129] Herb Altmann, interview by John Perdue, Kitchener, ON, December 29, 2011, recording in SOLIA.

[130] Lucille Ryan, letter to Frank Ryan, December 17, 1991. This letter is in the possession of Mr. Tom Ryan. Ryan travelled with his sisters Lucille, Bernie and Mary, and Mary's husband Walter (DHA, Father W.L. Ryan personnel file, letter from Father Ryan to Bishop Tonnos, Aug. 30,

Father Ryan was in good health and did not want to retire when his seventy-fifth birthday arrived in 1992,[131] but in obedience to his bishop at the time, the Most Reverend Anthony Tonnos, he stepped down from his position as pastor of St. Clement's Church on June 24, 1992[132] and moved to a bungalow at 526 Lancaster Street West in Kitchener, ON. There he received permission to reserve the Blessed Sacrament in a small chapel,[133] and a community of his friends would regularly come for Mass and breakfast. This time is remembered very fondly by those who attended. Father Ryan would hear confessions, offer the sacrifice of the Mass, spend long periods in prayer and offer spiritual direction.[134] At this time, too, Ryan was a member of the Nocturnal Adoration Society, whose members committed themselves to worshipping Our Lord in the Blessed Sacrament while

---

1991). See Appendix F for an image of the Ryan tombstone in Ireland with Father Ryan's name inscribed upon it.

[131] Patricia White and Janet Pfaffinger, interview by John Perdue, St. Clements, ON, December 28, 2011 recording in SOLIA.

[132] DHA, Father W.L. Ryan personnel file, letter from Bishop Tonnos to Father Ryan, March 24, 1992

[133] DHA, Father W.L. Ryan personnel file, letter from Father Ryan to Bishop Tonnos, June 15, 1992

[134] Herb Altmann, interview by John Perdue, Kitchener, ON, December 29, 2011, recording in SOLIA.

the world was asleep.[135] Indeed, Ryan remained very active in his retirement years, offering Mass for any congregations of religious sisters who requested him to do so[136] and regularly filling in for pastors during their vacation.[137]

In 2002, the owner of Father Ryan's house on Lancaster Street decided to sell the property, and Father moved into the Marian Residence at 640 Hillview Road, Cambridge, Ontario in June of that year.[138] This is the convent and retirement home of the Sisters of Our Lady Immaculate (SOLI) community. There, Father Ryan provided the Sacraments and spiritual direction for the sisters and for any friends and former parishioners who came to see him. He also continued to offer Sunday Mass at the Carmel of St. Joseph in Saint Agatha, ON. At this time, too, Ryan regularly attended a prayer vigil for an end to abortion that was held during the night in front of the Grand River Hospital in Kitchener. He continued in this

---

[135] Herb Altmann, interview by John Perdue, Kitchener, ON, December 29, 2011, recording in SOLIA.

[136] Father Loyd Ryan, letter to Frank Ryan, 1993 (exact date not specified). This letter is in the possession of Mr. Tom Ryan.

[137] On the weekend of August 22, 1999, for example, Father Ryan was filling in at the Church of St. Boniface in Maryhill, ON, and celebrated four Sunday Masses; two on Saturday evening and two on Sunday morning. He was 82 years old at the time. (SOLIA, Father Ryan homilies, Binder 31, August 22, 1999).

[138] DHA, Father W.L. Ryan personnel file, letter from Father Ryan to Bishop Tonnos May 9, 2002.

practice despite the concerns of some that his outings might be too taxing on his health.[139] Ryan, now 85 years old and fighting prostate cancer, was admitted to Cambridge Memorial Hospital on January 29, 2003 with urinary retention and a urinary tract infection.[140]

Several eyewitnesses have shared their memories of the final days and hours of Father Ryan's life. At different times he would recite the stations of the cross or say parts of the Mass, and he would regularly blurt out short prayers or Scripture passages – "they have pierced my hands and my feet, they have numbered all my bones!" He died on February 18, 2003 from complications due to pneumonia and prostate cancer.[141] Patti White and Janet Pfaffinger recall that when Father Ryan was laid in his coffin, so many people touched their rosaries to his body - considering him to be a saint[142] – that Father Robert Sims, Ryan's successor at St. Clement's parish, had to call the undertaker to have Father Ryan's hand re-positioned in his coffin.[143] As he had in life, so in

---

[139] Father Patric D'Arcy, telephone interview by John Perdue, Scarborough, ON, October 26, 2012, recording in SOLIA.

[140] SOLIA, Father Ryan medical records.

[141] DHA, Father W.L. Ryan personnel file. Father Ryan died at 7:40 in the morning.

[142] See Appendix G for a story attributing a miraculous healing to the intercessory prayer of Father Ryan.

[143] Patricia White and Janet Pfaffinger, interview by John Perdue, St. Clements, ON, December 28, 2011, recording in SOLIA.

death, Father Ryan continued to raise minds and hearts to God.

Chapter 2

Father Ryan and Priestly Vocations

Introduction

Having been introduced to Father William Loyd Ryan, we may now turn our attention to the central focus of this paper – Father Ryan's role in fostering priestly and religious vocations in the diocese of Hamilton. Firstly, as regards priestly vocations, it was Ryan's strong priestly identity that made it possible for him to survive the tumultuous 1960s and 1970s and the notable exodus from priestly ministry that occurred during these years. It was this identity, too, that made him an inspiration to young men considering vocations to the priesthood. Ryan's priesthood was balanced and grounded. In his mind the priest, like Christ, was meant to bridge the gap between God and humanity, allowing both the supernatural and the human elements of his mission to shine through.

During the 1940s and 1950s, Ryan's success in promoting vocations was attributable to his warmth and humanity. Young men were attracted to him because of his joy, because he played sports with them and because he took them camping and fishing. During the 1960s and 1970s, however, those men who identify Father Ryan as a positive influence in their decisions to become priests point to the more transcendent aspects of his ministry as the chief reasons that they admired him. His priestly identity, then, was at the heart of Father Ryan's success in fostering priestly vocations. At a time when the humanity of the priesthood was underemphasized, he allowed his humanity to shine through; when the supernatural aspect of priestly ministry needed affirmation, Ryan let this dimension of his vocation radiate. His balanced conception of the priest as *alter Christus* enabled attention to be drawn to either the human or the sacred facet of priestly ministry, depending on what young men needed in the given cultural milieu.

Father Ryan's Image of the Priesthood

Ryan began concretely shaping his image of what it meant to be a priest during his time at St. Augustine's Seminary. There, he kept a journal that included, among other things, many practical guidelines he laid out for his future self – guidelines and resolutions to ensure that he became a priest after the Heart of Christ. The essence of his observations on the priesthood during this time is expressed in the following quotation:

> It is of extreme necessity that a priest
> be holy and perfect. This is evident,
> from the high dignity of his office,
> his dignity as an "alter Christus," an

> imitation and personification of
> Christ, whose place he takes and who
> was all-perfect.[144]

Ryan saw the priest as an *alter Christus* – another Christ – called to live a life like His. And at the heart of Christ's identity, of course, is the *incarnation*. Jesus served as a bridge between God and humanity by the union, in His person, of humanity and divinity. The priest, called to continue the ministry of Christ on earth, must likewise bridge the gap between the people of his parish and God the Father. Ryan understood that he was called to be a warm and inviting man of the people, and simultaneously to offer the Sacraments for their sanctification. This image of the priesthood resonates throughout his seminary journal, where he makes several concrete resolutions aimed at helping him to live out the spiritual and the human dimensions of his ministry.[145]

There is evidence, too, that Ryan did not treat his resolutions flippantly. Father Clarence Hauser, C.R. (1916-2009) served at Father Ryan's confessor and spiritual director from 1987 until the time of Father Ryan's death in 2003.[146] Ryan told Father

---

[144] SOLIA, Father Ryan's seminary journal.

[145] See Appendix H for several revealing excerpts from Ryan's seminary journal.

[146] Father Clarence Hauser, C.R., interview by John Perdue, Waterloo, ON, December 31, 2009, recording in SOLIA. Before Father Hauser, Father Ryan went to Father Theodore Sobisch, C.R. for confession and spiritual

Hauser that he made an earnest effort to live up to the resolutions he had made as a seminarian. Father Hauser commented that if anything, Father Ryan was too hard on himself when he failed to live up to his ideals.[147] Here was a man who did not lose his priestly zeal.

Father Ryan saw the priest as a man who was prayerful, faithful, humble, obedient, merciful, hardworking, happy, firm when needed, and disposed to the will of God. The priest, for him, was a man who had put on Christ and whose primary task was to bring Christ to the people in the Eucharist. His image of the priesthood conforms very well to what has been called the 'cultic' model of the priesthood. According to this model, the priest's main task is to provide the people of God with the Sacraments, primarily Mass and confession. The priest lives a life distinguished by his consecration and concretely identified by his celibacy, his rectory life and his clerical garb. The priest leads and sanctifies the lay faithful.[148]

---

direction. When Father Sobisch died on March 30, 1987, Father Hauser became Father Ryan's spiritual director.

[147] SOLIA, Father Loyd Ryan, seminary journal: "It is of extreme necessity that a priest be holy and perfect...what then are his obligations as regards sanctity? Namely this, that always, no matter how holy and perfect he may think he is now, he must always seek to become more holy and more perfect. The minute he thinks he is holy enough and need not strive for greater sanctity, then does he begin to fall back".

[148] James J. Bacik, "The Practice of Priesthood: Working Through Today's Tensions" in *Priesthood in the Modern*

Father Patric D'Arcy surmises that it was Father Ryan's strong image of the priesthood that enabled him to preserve his vocation in the midst of the crisis in priestly identity following Vatican II and the shocking exodus from priestly ministry of many of Father Ryan's brother priests.[149] During this period, there was a sense among priests that their ministry was likely to change considerably, conforming more closely to what has been called the 'servant-leader' model of priestly ministry.[150] This model emphasizes the relationship between the ordained priest and the faith community. Priests share the human condition of all the faithful and participate in the office of Christ, the servant-head of the Church.[151] Some priests expected significant aspects of their priestly lives to change, with such possible adaptations as the introduction of optional celibacy.[152] Father Ryan did not subscribe to any of these beliefs, holding firmly

---

World, ed. Karen Sue Smith (Franklin, Wis: Sheed and Ward, 1999), 51-65.

[149] Father Patric D'Arcy, telephone interview by John Perdue, Scarborough, ON, October 26, 2012, recording in SOLIA. The Vatican's *Tabularum statisticarum collectio* of 1969 and *Annuarium statisticum Ecclesiae* of 1976 indicate that in that seven year period the number of priests fell globally from 413,000 to 343,000.

[150] Dean R. Hoge and Jacqueline E. Wenger, *Evolving Visions of the Priesthood: Changes from Vatican II to the Turn of the New Century* (Collegeville, Minn: Liturgical Press, 2003), 11.

[151] Bacik, 54.

[152] Hoge and Wenger, 8.

instead to the image of the priesthood that he had been exposed to as a child, that his seminary formation had prepared him for and that he had lived for the first twenty-five years of his priesthood.

Then came the publication of *Humanae Vitae* in 1968 and the widespread realization that some things would not change after all, such as the church's teaching on birth control.[153] This was somewhat of a watershed moment for the Church, ending much of the speculation and false hope that various priests had entertained about the future of their ministry and their expectations of sweeping reforms in the Church.[154] Some were disillusioned because their expectations were not realized, and some were floundering to find themselves, due to what they considered to be an unclear theology of the priesthood presented in the Vatican II document *Presbyterorum Ordinis* (Decree on the Ministry and Life of Priests).[155]

Of course, there were many factors that contributed to the general confusion regarding priestly identity and the subsequent exodus from priestly ministry. For one thing, lay ministry was strongly encouraged, which took some of the emphasis away from the pastoral role of the priest. The introduction

---

[153] Pope Paul VI, *Humanae Vitae* (Of Human Life), July 25, 1968, www.vatican.va.
[154] Ibid.
[155] Hoge and Wenger, 9; Pope Paul VI *Presbyterorum Ordinis* (Decree on the Ministry and Life of Priests), December 7, 1965, www.vatican.va.

of lay ministers of Holy Communion and the removal of the altar rail from churches physically symbolized the blurring of roles that was taking place in the minds of many of the faithful.[156] It is noteworthy, therefore, that Ryan did not remove the altar rail from the Church of Our Lady in Guelph, where he was stationed from 1969 to 1979, and that he encouraged his congregation to continue receiving Holy Communion kneeling and on the tongue. Indeed, there is considerable evidence that Father Ryan was uncomfortable with the progression of the liturgical reforms called for by the Second Vatican Council. As one interviewee put it, he felt that Ryan never quite "graduated" to Vatican II.[157]

Even in the face of Ryan's resistance to the changes going on around him, though, it is unfair to characterize his decisions as gestures of resistance to the reforms of Vatican II.[158] It is more accurate to say that they represented resistance to the *implementation*

---

[156] Hoge and Wenger, 11.

[157] Father Phillip Sherlock, interview by John Perdue, Cambridge, ON, December 27, 2011, recording in SOLIA.

[158] For example, Father Ryan retained the use of the chalice veil and the burse, he only permitted male lectors and altar servers and (with the permission of Bishop Tonnos) he introduced the celebration of the Tridentine Mass at St. Clement's Church in St. Clements in 1990. Father Ryan began offering the Tridentine Mass weekly at the Carmel of St. Agatha in St. Agatha, on June 28th, 1992 (SOLIA, Sisters of Our Lady Immaculate, *Who is the Priest?,* digital slideshow, produced by the Sisters of Our Lady Immaculate, 2003).

of the reforms of the Council, which Father Ryan saw progressing incorrectly or too quickly in many parts of the country. For his part, Ryan had a very positive take on the reforms themselves, referring to *Sacrosanctum Concilium*, [159] for example, as "the excellent constitution on the liturgy," and lauding the reforms it mandated. [160] In response to those who labeled him 'pre-Vatican II', Ryan would say "as Cardinal Ratzinger has said, there is no such thing as a pre-Vatican Church and a post-Vatican Church: it is the same one Church, which goes back to Christ and the Apostles." [161]

We may take, as an example, the fact that Father Ryan continued to wear his cassock and biretta when the vast majority of clerics in Canada had adopted black dress pants and a black clerical shirt as ordinary clerical attire. This certainly demonstrates a stubborn attachment to tradition and a resistance to conformity. It does not, however, contravene any ecclesiastical ruling, either from the documents of Vatican II, from the CCCB or from the diocese of Hamilton. Father Ryan was a very obedient man who adhered strictly to the Magisterium of the Church. It was undoubtedly an aid to Ryan that his bishop during the Vatican II era was Joseph F. Ryan, who is

---

[159] Pope Paul VI, *Sacrosanctum Concilium* (Constitution on the Sacred Liturgy), July 25, 1968, www.vatican.va.
[160] SOLIA, Father Ryan's homilies, Binder 24.
[161] SOLIA, Father Ryan's homilies, Binder 20.

commonly regarded – sometimes unfairly[162] – as one of the most stubborn resisters to reform in Canada in the post-Vatican II era.

According to the standards of the 1960s and 1970s, then, Father Ryan was certainly extreme in his adherence to the liturgical traditions under which he had been formed. But his success in preserving the liturgical and pastoral elements of his ministry which he considered important undoubtedly contributed to the preservation of his priestly identity. In defense of his efforts to cling to externals such as the use of a chalice veil and burse and the wearing of the cassock and biretta, Ryan would likely point to Jesus' words "He who is faithful in a very little is faithful also in much" (Lk. 16:10).

Of course, though, externals such as clerical garb and liturgical linens were not the rock on which Ryan's priestly identity was built. Rather, as his many homilies on vocations demonstrate, he had firm beliefs about the bedrock on which the edifice of priestly life must be built. They reveal Father Ryan's determined reliance on prayer, on the Mass and devotion to Jesus in the Blessed Sacrament, on an ever-deepening love for the Blessed Virgin Mary, and his unbreakable loyalty to the pope.[163] These, for Ryan, were means of assuring the perseverance of

---

[162] Bishop Matthew Ustrzycki, telephone interview by John Perdue, Guelph, ON, August 18, 2013.
[163] SOLIA, Father Loyd Ryan, homily for Vocations Sunday, April 16, 1978, Father Ryan's homilies, Binder 14.

priests and religious in their vocations. Always aware of the need to lead by example, Ryan constantly availed himself of these means to holiness and to the preservation of one's vocation, and in doing so, remained faithful to his vocation until death.

Ryan was also deeply aware of the importance of priestly fraternity. He knew that a priest, like any human being, has a need for lasting friendships. And when a priest can find fellowship with a brother priest, he meets the human need for companionship and simultaneously encourages his own priestly identity. [164] Ryan maintained several lifelong friendships with brother priests who shared his joys and sorrows, assisted in his pastoral endeavours and joined him in recreation. [165] Preeminent among his priest confreres was Father Aloysius Nolan (1917-1983), a priest of the London diocese whom Ryan met in 1942, just one month after Nolan's ordination. They became fast friends, and both parishioners and family members of Father Ryan remember Nolan arriving by motorcycle and

---

[164] See Emile Briere, *Priests Need Priests* (Combermere: Madonna House Publications, 1992).

[165] Mary Clare also remembers Father Ryan maintaining a friendship with Father John Carley of the Archdiocese of Kingston, whom Father Ryan met during his seminary years (Mary Clare, interview by John Perdue, Goderich, ON, November 21, 2009, recording in SOLIA). Father Wayne Lobsinger recalls Father Ryan's close friendship with Father Vincent Shea (Father Wayne Lobsinger, interview by John Perdue, Waterdown, ON, November 6, 2012, recording in SOLIA).

accompanying Ryan on hunting and fishing trips, on visits to parishioners' homes, on trips with altar servers and on visits to parish missions.[166] Both the human and the transcendent aspects of Father Ryan's priesthood were nourished by the lifelong friendships he maintained with his confreres.

At this point we can step back and evaluate what we have identified as the bulwarks of Father Ryan's priestly identity. At its heart, Ryan saw the priesthood as the call to be another Christ – to mediate between God and humankind. He identified with what has been called the 'cultic' model of the priesthood. From the earliest years of his formation, he had a strong awareness of the centrality of the Sacraments and the liturgy in the life of a priest. He firmly believed that a life of prayer, devotion to the Blessed Sacrament and to the Blessed Virgin Mary and the rigorous maintenance of any external habit or devotion that fostered priestly identity were important in the living out of a priestly vocation. The priest, for Ryan, had also to be warm and approachable in order to bridge effectively the gap between God and humanity. Finally, Ryan valued priestly fraternity as a means of sustaining his vocation and that of his brothers in the presbyterate. These are among the tools that enabled Father Ryan to

---

[166] Mary Clare, interview by John Perdue, Goderich, ON, November 21, 2009, recording in SOLIA; Paul Ryan, interview by John Perdue, North Brant, ON, October 24, 2012, recording in SOLIA.

live out his vocation faithfully and to be recognized as a priest "through and through."[167]

Ryan's Influence in Fostering Priestly Vocations

Having looked at his image of the priesthood, we turn our attention now to Father Ryan's role in fostering vocations. Ryan had success in promoting vocations to the priesthood throughout the duration of his priestly ministry, which spanned sixty-three years and some very tumultuous times within and without the Church. But an interesting shift can be noted in the locus of Ryan's fruitfulness in fostering vocations before and after the Second Vatican Council: whereas before the Council, aspirants to the priesthood were drawn to his inviting human qualities, afterwards, young men were attracted to his profound spiritual and devotional life. As we have seen, both of these aspects were part of the single, solidly rooted priestly identity that Ryan had cultivated. But young men were drawn to one or the other aspect of Ryan's priesthood depending upon the prevailing cultural ethos. At no time were they naïve about either the human or the spiritual character of the priesthood, but Ryan's balanced priestly identity allowed them to be

---

[167] Gerry Doucette, interview by John Perdue, Cambridge, ON, December 29, 2011, recording in SOLIA.

drawn to whatever facet of the priesthood they needed to see emphasized.

Before examining the shift that took place in Father Ryan's promotion of priestly vocations, it will be helpful to outline those aspects of his approach to fostering vocations which never changed. The only recorded directive of Our Lord concerning vocations is the admonition "Pray, therefore, the Lord of the harvest, that He may send labourers into His harvest" (Mt. 9:38). Ryan took this admonition seriously and prayed regularly for an increase in vocations to the priesthood and the religious life. Ryan's daily prayers included petitions for an increase in vocations.[168] In his homilies, too, there is evidence of Ryan's prayerful concern for vocations. He regularly asked his parishioners to pray for vocations, and his efforts increased when an ordination was forthcoming.[169]

Ryan also firmly believed that an emphasis on the happiness and the sacredness of priestly ministry was essential in efforts to promote vocations. In 1951, he gave a talk on vocations to students in grades six, seven and eight.[170] From his preparatory notes, it is clear that Ryan considered it very important to emphasize the happiness of a priestly or religious

---

[168] Gerry Doucette, interview by John Perdue, Cambridge, ON, December 29, 2011, recording in SOLIA.

[169] SOLIA, Father Loyd Ryan, notes for Vocations Awareness Week, April 28-May 5th, 1985, Father Ryan homilies, Binder 20.

[170] SOLIA, Father Loyd Ryan, preparatory notes, December 7, 1951, Father Ryan's homilies, Folder 'A' package 'A.2'.

vocation, and what a privilege it was to help God in His mission. Father Ryan emphasized the personal dimension of the call, highlighting the awesomeness of the fact that God wants *you* to help Him. Father calls the life of a priest a "hard one, but a glorious one." In some of his sermons, he encouraged the children to ask any priest or religious if they would ever give up their state of life for a life in the world. Ryan clearly believed that to do so would be unthinkable.[171]

When Ryan spoke to his congregations about fostering vocations, he repeatedly returned to the same themes. Firstly, he stressed that the faith in our homes must be strengthened. The family environment needed to be one that allowed the seeds of a vocation to take root. Secondly, vocations must be fostered by teachers in Catholic schools – schoolchildren should be taught about the happiness of religious life and the priesthood, beginning at an early age. Thirdly, parishes and schools ought to establish vocations clubs. Above all else, though, as has been mentioned, Father always emphasized prayer.[172]

Ryan considered it to be a good thing that many young men should go to the seminary. He believed that a young man need not be sure whether he is called or not, because his time in seminary

---

[171] SOLIA, Father Loyd Ryan, preparatory notes for a talk on vocations, undated (suspected to have been composed in 1951), Father Ryan's homilies, Folder 'A' package 'A.2'.
[172] Ibid.

would not be wasted, and it would become clear to him whether or not he had a call as he moved through formation.[173] Time in seminary afforded young men a unique opportunity for discernment that was worthy of any thoughtful person, regardless of the outcome. When speaking to young men or women who believed they had a call to the priesthood or religious life, Ryan recommended that they talk about it with their families and with their parish priest or a religious brother or sister, that they pray about it regularly, and that they attend Mass regularly – daily, if possible.[174]

Having outlined some of the perennial aspects of Ryan's approach to fostering priestly vocations, attention can now be paid to the shift that took place in the locus of his fruitfulness in vocational promotion. As has been mentioned, the young men whose vocations were encouraged by Father Ryan in the 1940s and 1950s were inspired by the human qualities that shone through in his pastoral praxis, while the young men who were inspired by Father Ryan in the years from 1960 to 2000 were impressed by his strong priestly identity and the image of the priesthood of Jesus Christ that he provided. This shift in the source of Ryan's success in promoting

---

[173] SOLIA, Father Loyd Ryan, preparatory notes for a talk on vocations, undated (suspected to have been composed in 1951), Father Ryan's homilies, Folder 'A' package 'A.2'.
[174] SOLIA, Father Loyd Ryan, notes for Vocations Awareness Week, April 28–May 5th, 1985, Father Ryan homilies, Binder 20.

vocations was occasioned by the cultural and ecclesial changes of the 1960s. The uncertainty that ensued made Father Ryan somewhat of a beacon to those seeking stability and groundedness in the priesthood.

In the 1940s and 1950s, when Father Ryan was a newly ordained priest, the practice of the Catholic faith in the Hamilton diocese was robust. The population of Catholics was expanding at a remarkable rate due to a heavy influx of immigrants from war-devastated Europe and to an unusually high birth rate.[175] Under the direction of Bishop Ryan, many new churches and schools were built to accommodate the rapid population increase. Weekly Mass attendance was high; religious confraternities fostered the faith of the lay faithful; popular piety was sustained by vigorous devotional lives; and the Catholic faith was at the heart of the social life of many families.[176] At this time, too, the priesthood was deeply respected. In the minds of many lay faithful, priests were revered authority figures, distinguished by their special power to celebrate the Sacraments.[177]

In this context, the welcoming and jovial demeanor that Ryan brought to his ministry helped young men to see that the priesthood was not

---

[175] Ken Foyster, *Anniversary Reflections: A History of the Hamilton Diocese (1856-1981)* (Hamilton: W.L. Griffin Ltd., 1981), 38.

[176] Ibid., 40.

[177] David L. Toups, *Reclaiming Our Priestly Character* (Omaha: Institute for Priestly Formation Publications, 2010), xvi.

64

inaccessible to them. His efforts at fostering vocations involved lively and entertaining trips with his altar boys. These outings gave Father Ryan an opportunity to demonstrate the joy in his own heart, and also to get to know the boys outside of the parish setting. While he was associate pastor at Sacred Heart Church in Guelph in the 1940s, Ryan and his friend Father Nolan would take groups of young men whom they suspected might have vocations and go hunting and fishing with them.[178] Father Ryan's sister, Mary Clare, remembers large groups of altar servers coming up to the Ryan homestead in North Brant for a weekend of hunting, fishing, swimming and sleeping in the hay mow.[179] Father Ryan was constantly introducing the young people in his life to priests and religious, which no doubt opened their eyes to the possibility that they, too, might become priests or religious.[180]

While Father Ryan was associate pastor to Monsignor Peter Moloney at St. Mary's Church in Brantford from 1947 to 1958 "a whole raft" of young men went from that parish to the seminary.[181] Father

---

[178] Father Harry Schmuck, telephone interview by John Perdue, Douro, ON, December 21, 2011, transcript in SOLIA.

[179] Mary Clare, interview by John Perdue, Goderich, ON, November 21, 2009, recording in SOLIA.

[180] Paul Ryan, interview by John Perdue, North Brant, ON, October 24, 2012, recording in SOLIA.

[181] Father Harry Schmuck, telephone interview by John Perdue, Douro, ON, December 21, 2011, transcript in SOLIA.

Ryan undoubtedly had an influence on many of them.[182] Among these young men were five boys from the Sherlock family, of whom two became priests (Fathers William and Phillip Sherlock) and a third became bishop of the London diocese, John-Michael Sherlock. John Sherlock was twenty-one years old and already in First Theology when Father Ryan arrived as curate at St. Mary's.[183] As their father was the church's caretaker at the time, the boys spent a great deal of time with Father Ryan. John and Phil remember that all of the Sherlock boys were very enthusiastic concerning Father Ryan, as were most of the boys in town.[184] Ryan did not have a car at the time, so he rode his bicycle around town, acting as somewhat of a hero to many of the youngsters. Bishop Sherlock remembers his mother telling him "if you are as good a priest as Father Ryan, I will be very proud of you."

Ryan impressed the family – and the community – as a man of profound faith and overflowing joy. Both Sherlock brothers served on the altar for Ryan and attended his altar-server trips to the

---

[182] Father Harry Schmuck, telephone interview by John Perdue, Douro, ON, December 21, 2011, transcript in SOLIA.

[183] Bishop John-Michael Sherlock, telephone interview by John Perdue, Peterborough, ON, March 26, 2012, transcript in SOLIA. Everything pertaining to Bishop John-Michael Sherlock has been drawn from this interview.

[184] Father Phillip Sherlock, interview by John Perdue, Cambridge, ON, December 27, 2011, recording in SOLIA.

family farm in North Brant. For Father Phil, considering a priestly vocation came quite naturally due to his brother John's example. Ryan, though, provided an encouraging example of the life he was considering. Both Sherlock brothers point to Father Ryan's holy life and his joy as the factors that combined to make him a tremendous inspiration.

Bishop Matthew Ustrzycki and his brothers also served on the altar for Father Ryan when he was associate pastor at Sacred Heart in Guelph during the Second World War.[185] Bishop Ustrzycki was in grade six at the time, and recalls that Ryan made an impression on the boys because he was a good hockey player, and played often with the boys. He helped them to build a large rink in the schoolyard, where they marveled at how Ryan "skated like the wind." Like many other men whose lives were touched by Father Ryan, Bishop Ustrzycki acknowledges him as an influence in his decision to enter seminary. Ryan was not a forceful or imposing character, but his mild-mannered, holy way of life and his love for the priesthood fed a growing desire in the young man's heart.[186]

Before examining Father Ryan's influence in fostering vocations after the Second Vatican Council, it will be important to outline a few of the primary cultural shifts that caused a man of firm identity and

---

[185] Bishop Matthew Ustrzycki, interview by John Perdue, Guelph, ON, December 29, 2011, recording in SOLIA.
[186] Ibid.

67

resoluteness to become a relative rarity. The shifts in priestly identity that followed the Council, while certainly pertinent, have already been outlined. Culturally, the western world of the 1960s demonstrated at least four over-arching shifts. There was a greater sense of pluralism and a recognition of differing cultures and traditions, a generally declining trust in institutions, more open and more widely tolerated sexual behaviour and a shift from hierarchically to collegially structured organizations.[187] The 1960s inaugurated a time of innovation, progress and questioning. In many circles it became somewhat unfashionable to believe in objective truth or to subscribe to the beliefs of an organized religion. Both culturally and ecclesially, then, Ryan began to stand out. He was a man who valued tradition, hierarchy, order and institutions. The changes going on around him and his response to these changes made him a figure who drew attention.

Among those whose attention Father Ryan attracted during this period are several priests and bishops who acknowledge him as a positive influence in their decision to enter the seminary. Ryan was Thomas Collins' parish priest at the Church of Our Lady in Guelph when the beginnings of a priestly vocation were stirring in his heart. It was to Father Ryan that Thomas expressed his interest, and Father Ryan directed him to Bishop Reding. Thomas would

---

[187] Hoge and Wenger, 16-18.

go on to become priest, Bishop, Archbishop, and ultimately the Cardinal Archbishop of Toronto. Cardinal Collins describes Ryan as "quiet, holy and prayerful. He was a good example of priestly virtue."[188] Cardinal Collins and his sister, Catharine, both recall Collins serving Mass for Father Ryan. Cardinal Collins acknowledges Father Ryan as an example of priestly virtue who formed his image of the priesthood and fostered his desire to answer the call. Father Ryan, as Collins' parish priest, was present at his ordination and his First Mass.[189]

Father Wayne Lobsinger's association with Father Ryan began in the fall of 1984, when Ryan was pastor at St. Clement's Church in St. Clements, Ontario.[190] Lobsinger, who was in grade thirteen at the time, applied for a position as organist. At the end of a fifteen-minute interview, Father Ryan said "thank you, but no." Reminiscing lightheartedly on the encounter, Father Lobsinger speculates that Father Ryan likely felt that such a young man would not be well enough versed in ecclesial music to function as organist and choir director. Shortly thereafter,

---

[188] Thomas Cardinal Collins, interview by John Perdue, Scarborough, ON, November 14, 2012, transcript in SOLIA.

[189] See Appendix I for a picture of Thomas Collins' Mass of Thanksgiving after his ordination to the priesthood.

[190] Father Wayne Lobsinger, interview by John Perdue, Waterdown, ON, November 6, 2012, recording in SOLIA. Everything pertaining to Father Wayne Lobsinger has been drawn from this interview.

however, Lobsinger received a call from his great aunt, who was in the choir at St. Clement's and who had spoken to Father Ryan. She informed Lobsinger that he had gotten the job after all. It was his responsibility to run the Thursday choir practice and play for the 10:30 Sunday Mass, and also the Christmas and Easter Masses. So began a relationship that would last until Father Ryan's death in 2003.

Lobsinger was playing the organ at St. Clement's Forty Hours Devotion in the fall of 1985 when the guest homilist spoke about his own vocation to the priesthood. It was at that moment that the thought struck him – "like a bolt from the blue" – that he should become a priest. Father Ryan was the first person Lobsinger spoke to about this. He and Ryan had grown quite close through their constant association over matters liturgical and personal. Lobsinger considered Ryan to be a man of prayer and a priest after the heart of Christ, and he respected him for that. It was when Bishop Matthew Ustrzycki, the auxiliary Bishop for the diocese of Hamilton at the time, came to St. Clement's for confirmations in the spring of 1986 that Ryan arranged for a meeting between Lobsinger and Bishop Ustrzycki. Lobsinger applied to the seminary, and began his studies in the fall of 1986. He acknowledges Father Ryan as the main influence in his own priestly vocation, and his description of Ryan's influence draws particular attention to Ryan's spiritual life.

Ryan and Lobsinger maintained their relationship throughout Lobsinger's formation. While he was completing his philosophy studies at St. Jerome's in Waterloo, Lobsinger returned every Sunday to St. Clement's to serve at benediction and lead the rosary for the parish Holy Hour. He remembers sitting and visiting with Father Ryan after the weekly Holy Hour, and acknowledges that his vocation was fostered by Father Ryan's kindness and the example of his profound relationship with God. Lobsinger recognized Father Ryan's strong priestly identity, and this influenced him profoundly as he began to discern his call seriously.

Before Father Patric D'Arcy had entered the seminary, he remembers Ryan filling in for Father Vernon Cullaton at St. Clement's Church in Preston in the 1990s. Father D'Arcy would get to know Father Ryan much better later in life, through mutual friends. D'Arcy says that Ryan's faithfulness to his breviary, his strong priestly character and example and his obvious love for the Mass all greatly encouraged him in his own discernment. He particularly remembers being inspired by Father Ryan's obvious identification with the priesthood of Jesus Christ. He was aware that many priests had lost their identity and subsequently their vocation in the 1960s and 70s, so he appreciated

Ryan's awareness of who he was and what he was meant to do – he was to be another Christ.[191]

Father D'Arcy happily acknowledges Ryan as a role model in his own priesthood, and feels that any seminarian or priest would do himself a service in taking Father Ryan as an example. D'Arcy says Ryan's influence in fostering priestly vocations flowed from the example of his life. He believes Christ gave us the blueprint for holiness in the evangelical counsels of poverty, chastity and obedience, and Ryan's influence on vocations stemmed from the degree to which he lived these counsels, thereby identifying with Christ. Father Ryan pointed to Heaven and to something beyond himself, giving inspiration to others who might have a vocation, particularly to the priesthood.

We have seen, then, that in the early days of Ryan's priestly ministry – the golden years of the priesthood in North America – young men aspiring to Holy Orders were drawn to his human traits. He was jovial and amiable with them and he took groups of them fishing and swimming and camping. With the cultural and ecclesial shifts of the 1960s, however, the locus of Ryan's effectiveness in fostering vocations shifted. The chief source of inspiration for young men was no longer the friendliness, joviality or sportiness of their priests. Instead, they were hungry for

---

[191] Father Patric D'Arcy, telephone interview by John Perdue, Scarborough, ON, October 26, 2012, recording in SOLIA.

examples of strong priestly character at a time when the nature of the ministerial priesthood was unclear in many minds. They wanted to see men who were deeply spiritual and unwavering in their commitment to Christ and the Church. Because Ryan had deeply appropriated who he was as a priest – that he was a man called act in the person of Christ the head – he provided a light that attracted young men considering vocations in two very different cultural and ecclesial contexts.

Chapter 3

Father Ryan and the Founding of the Sisters of Our Lady Immaculate

Introduction

Having explored the role that priestly identity played in the life and ministry of Father Loyd Ryan, we turn our attention now to the role of identity in his efforts to promote vocations to consecrated religious life in the diocese of Hamilton. Just as he had understood the primacy of identity in his priestly ministry, Father Ryan similarly recognized the need for consecrated religious to be firmly grounded in who they were and what it meant to be given over to Christ through the vows of poverty, chastity and obedience. His convictions in this regard impelled him to action when many women's religious orders were struggling to find their identity and were subsequently losing vocations in the tumultuous 1960s and 1970s. As Ryan's strong priestly character had become a beacon to young men considering vocations to the priesthood, so would his vision of consecrated religious life become a beacon to disaffected consecrated women religious and to young women considering vocations to religious life during this tumultuous period. The result? A new congregation of women religious in the diocese of Hamilton, the Sisters of Our Lady Immaculate.

Before identifying the cultural and ecclesial shifts that motivated Father Ryan to found a new congregation of women religious, it will be important to establish his image of religious life. Ryan himself had considered a religious vocation, refraining from joining the Oblates of Mary Immaculate as a young man only because of the strong opposition of his mother. However he remained enamoured of consecrated religious life for the rest of his ministry, maintaining longstanding friendships with many consecrated women religious.[192] His familiarity with religious sisters began when he was a schoolboy in North Brant, where the Sisters of St. Joseph of Hamilton would visit during the summer months to acquire provisions to support their community.[193] As mentioned in Chapter One, Ryan's first elementary school teacher left her position to join that community in 1925.[194] During his priestly ministry, Ryan was appointed ordinary confessor to the Sisters of Notre Dame attached to the Hanover convent, and extraordinary confessor to the Walkerton and Owen Sound convents of the Sisters of Notre Dame on July 14th 1960.[195] The Sisters of St. Joseph of Hamilton

---

[192] Paul Ryan, interview by John Perdue, North Brant, ON, October 24, 2012, recording in SOLIA.

[193] Mary Fleming, telephone interview by John Perdue, Scarborough, ON, January 27, 2013, transcript in SOLIA.

[194] St. Michael's Church: North Brant, Ontario 1883-1983. [Hamilton]: 1983, 70.

[195] DHA, Bishop Reding file, letter from Bishop Reding to Father Ryan, June 16, 1960.

were ministering in Brantford when Ryan was associate pastor at St. Mary's from 1945 to 1947 and in Guelph during Ryan's term as pastor at the Church of Our Lady from 1969 to 1979.[196] Ryan's lifetime of ministry alongside consecrated sisters and his close friendship with many religious afforded him a certain familiarity with the pattern of life of various religious communities.[197]

Through these associations, Ryan had developed an image of what it meant to be a consecrated religious. At its most fundamental level, he saw religious life as a call to conformity with Christ – *Christ* was to be the identity of the religious sister. Ryan was anxious to have sisters understand that their first and foremost mission was to conform themselves to Christ, their spouse, and that this conformity would lend fruitfulness to any ministry they undertook. Interestingly, years before the idea of founding a religious community had entered his mind, Ryan had said – in words which would one day apply to himself – "The founders of Religious Orders practically always had this in mind. The rules vary in detail, but essentially, they all aim to help their members to imitate Our Lord – to reproduce Christ in themselves so that they could say, like St. Paul, *I live*

---

[196] SOLIA, Sister Doreen Kaminski, CSJ, *A brief history of Congregation of the Sisters of Saint Joseph in Hamilton*, given to John Perdue, January 24, 2013.
[197] Paul Ryan, interview by John Perdue, North Brant, ON, October 24, 2012, recording in SOLIA.

now, not I, but Christ lives in me."[198] This is the ideal of religious life to which Father Ryan subscribed.

The pillars of such a life, in Ryan's mind, were joyful community living centred on the Eucharist, a structured life of prayer in imitation of the Blessed Virgin Mary and a shared charism. These three pillars, together with external manifestations of the commitment to religious life, such as the habit,[199] would enable the consecrated religious to adhere faithfully to his or her vows of poverty, chastity and obedience. [200] This was Father Ryan's image of consecrated life, and, like his image of the priesthood, he clung to it tenaciously. Fortunately for Ryan, the life of most congregations of religious ministering in the diocese of Hamilton in the early years of his ministry conformed very closely to this paradigm. A tension would arise, however, in the 1960s and 1970s, when the image of religious life presented above – Ryan's image – would come under scrutiny and many orders would begin to modify their constitutions and their approaches to religious life.

---

[198] SOLIA, Father Loyd Ryan, homily to the School Sisters of Notre Dame in Walkerton, ON, October 1959, Father Ryan homilies, Binder 9.
[199] Mother St. Henry Moloney, SOLI, interview by John Perdue, Cambridge, ON, December 29, 2011, recording in SOLIA.
[200] Sister Joan McMahon, CSJ, interview by John Perdue, Dundas, ON, February 6, 2013, transcript in SOLIA.

Cultural and Ecclesial Changes

We saw above that the 1960s inaugurated a time of tremendous change both within and without the church. There are two areas of change, however, that are particularly relevant to our discussion of Ryan and women's religious life: education and renewal within women's religious congregations. Ryan's strong feelings about the transformations he saw taking place in these two areas compelled him to explore the possibility of founding a new community of women religious in the diocese of Hamilton in the 1970s. [201]

Under the guidance of William Davis, Ontario's Minister of Education, the Ontario education system underwent considerable changes in the 1960s. Davis commissioned the Hall-Dennis Report, which called for sweeping province-wide reforms in pedagogy.[202] Child-centered education took precedence over teacher-centered education, self-discipline over external discipline, learning-from-play over education-as-work and the discovery approach

---

[201] DHA, Sisters of Our Lady Immaculate file, letter from Bishop Reding to Sister Teresa Ann, March 10, 1977, file P36.007.007.

[202] The official title of the report was *Living and Learning: The Report of the Provincial Committee on Aims and Objectives of Education in the Schools of Ontario.*

over memorization and learning.[203] Buzzwords at the time were 'pupil choice', 'non-gradedness' and 'the needs and interests of the child'.[204] During the same year, Pope Paul VI promulgated the document *Gravissimum educationis.* [205] This document encouraged Christian teachers to be "carefully prepared so that both in secular and religious knowledge they are equipped with suitable qualifications and also with a pedagogical skill that is in keeping with the findings of the contemporary world."[206] Those responsible for Catholic education in Canada, having been encouraged to align their pedagogical approach with the findings of the contemporary world, understandably adopted a very subject-centered, discovery-style approach to catechesis. The result was the *Come to the Father* series, also known as the *Canadian Catechism*, published in 1972 under the guidance and direction of the Canadian Catholic Conference (later the Canadian

---

[203] Robert T. Dixon, *Catholic Education and Politics in Ontario Volume IV* (Toronto: Catholic Education Foundation of Ontario, 2003), 4.

[204] Ryan, we shall see, was not opposed to modernizing education and catechesis, but he was leery of the rapidity and severity of the changes. While a shift toward a more subject-centered approach was helpful, he regretted the accompanying tendency to underemphasize the importance of *content*.

[205] Pope Paul VI, *Gravissimum Educationis* (The Importance of Education), October 28, 1965, www.vatican.va.

[206] Ibid.

Conference of Catholic Bishops – CCCB). The *Come to the Father* series replaced the doctrinally heavy question-and-answer style of the *Baltimore Catechism* [207] with "an experiential, psychological, developmental approach geared to the age, interests and abilities of the child".[208] As we shall see, Father Ryan was among those who remained unconvinced that this shift in educational approach was helpful.

A final noteworthy development in education in Ontario in the 1960s was the exodus of women religious from Catholic schools. Teaching orders of women religious such as the Sisters of St. Joseph, the Institute of the Blessed Virgin Mary (IBVM), the School Sisters of Notre Dame and the Grey Sisters of the Immaculate Conception had been the backbone of the education system in Ontario until the 1960s. During this decade, however, a steep decline in religious vocations, the exclaustration of a number of teaching religious and the rapid expansion of the separate school system resulted in a staff made up almost entirely of laity. [209] Ontario Premier John Robarts, in response to massive post-War expansion and accompanying pressure from advocates of the separate school system, [210] announced the Ontario Foundation Tax Plan in February 1963. The Foundation Tax Plan placed the separate school

---

[207] Also known as *A Catechism of Christian Doctrine*.
[208] Dixon, 269.
[209] Ibid., 380.
[210] Including the Ontario Catholic bishops.

system in Ontario on an equal financial footing with the public school system,[211] making it possible for lay teachers to support a family with their wages. This and other political breakthroughs in the financing of separate schools, [212] coupled with Vatican II's promotion of the lay apostolate – especially in the 1965 document *Apostolicam Actuositatem* [213] – allowed for a relatively rapid movement from a consecrated religious-dominated separate school system to a layperson-dominated separate school system.

But the movement of women religious out of separate schools was not only the result of changes in education and the rise of the lay apostolate. Drastic changes in the life of women religious in Ontario – and throughout the world – contributed to the movement of sisters out of schools and into other forms of ministry. We turn our attention now to the renewal of religious life, the unfolding of which was the second impetus behind Father Ryan's movement to found a new congregation of women religious.[214]

---

[211] For a detailed description of the Foundation Tax Plan, see Dixon, 333-334.

[212] Dixon, Part IV, 325-371.

[213] Pope Paul VI, *Apostolicam Actuositatem* (Decree on the Apostolate of the Laity), November 18, 1965, www.vatican.va.

[214] What follows is a brief analysis of the reforms following Vatican II. Note, however, that the seeds of the reform of religious life had been planted years before the convocation of the Second Vatican Council, particularly during the papacy of Pope Pius XII. For a more detailed analysis of

A growing body of research describes the changes that took place within the life of women religious following the Second Vatican Council.[215] Before the reforms, members made vows of poverty, chastity and obedience and followed the Rules of their community. Rules governed their prayer and worship, work, enclosure, governance, dress, deportment, daily routines, dining and diet, spiritual reading, silence, recreation and rest.[216] Then, in 1965, Vatican II's *Perfectae Caritatis* (Decree on the Adaptation and Renewal of Religious Life)[217] encouraged consecrated religious to adapt their manner of living, praying, working and their mode of governance to suit the

---

the lead-up to the renewal of religious life, see R.D. Bondy, "Roman Catholic Women Religious and Organizational Reform in English Canada: The Ursuline and Holy Names Sisters in the Diocese of London, Ontario, 1950-1970" (Ph.D. diss., University of Waterloo, 2007), 51-71.

[215] For a look at reforms to Ontario's women's religious orders, see Rosa Bruno-Jofré's *The Missionary Oblate Sisters: Vision and Mission*, James Cameron's *And Martha Served: History of the Sisters of St. Martha*, Elizabeth Smyth and Linda Wicks' *Wisdom Raises Her Voice: The Sisters of St. Joseph of Toronto Celebrate 150 Years* or Mary Olga McKenna's *Charity Alive: The Sisters of Charity of St. Vincent de Paul, Halifax, 1950-1979.*

[216] For a more detailed treatment of the characteristics of women's religious congregations in Ontario before the reforms of the Second Vatican Council, see Bondy, 51-53.

[217] Pope Paul VI, *Perfectae Caritatis* (Decree on the Adaptation and Renewal of Religious Life), October 28, 1965, www.vatican.va.

changed conditions of the time.[218] Pope Paul VI called for the suitable re-editing of the constitutions, directories, custom books, books of prayer and ceremonies of religious orders, with obsolete laws being suppressed. [219] Congregations of women religious in Ontario zealously undertook the renewal of their communities.

Rosa Bruno-Jofré's description of renewal within the Missionary Oblate Sisters in Canada provides a window into the reform of Canadian congregations following Vatican II. During this time, the Missionary Oblates went through a "rapid and uneasy process of changing obsolete customs and traditions that affected daily life....Many of the structures of common life built upon observance of rules were discarded, among them taking recreation in common and the daily timetable. Sisters took back their secular names, modified the habit and then gradually began to wear secular clothes".[220] Little by little the rules governing what a sister could and could not own were modified, as were the rules governing the use of television, correspondence, visits, holidays and swimming. The sisters "began to question their

---

[218] Pope Paul VI, *Perfectae Caritatis* (Decree on the Adaptation and Renewal of Religious Life), October 28, 1965, www.vatican.va, 3.

[219] Ibid.

[220] Rosa Bruno-Jofré, "The Process of Renewal of the Missionary Oblate Sisters, 1963-1989" in *Changing Habits: Women's Religious Orders in Canada*, ed. Elizabeth M. Smyth (Ottawa: Novalis, 2007), 251-252.

vow of obedience with reference to assigned tasks".[221]

Most pertinent to our discussion of Father Ryan and the founding of the Sisters of Our Lady Immaculate, though, is the observation that the Missionary Oblate Sisters, like many other congregations of women religious at this time, experienced "a loss of identity and mission".[222] This loss of identity has been cited as the most significant contributing factor in the exodus of women from their religious congregations. [223] Jofré notes that the Missionary Oblate Sisters suffered many defections from their congregation. In this they were not alone – the number of women religious ministering in Father Ryan's home diocese of Hamilton dropped from 698 to 426 over the twenty-year period from 1972 to 1992.[224] Of all of the concerns Father Ryan had with respect to the renewal of religious life in Ontario, he most deeply regretted the loss of identity among women religious and their subsequent abandonment of religious life.

[221] Bruno-Jofré, *The Process of Renewal*, 252.

[222] Ibid., 251.

[223] John Padberg, S.J., "The Contexts of Comings and Goings" in *The Crisis in Religious Vocations: An Inside View*, ed. Laurie Felknor (New York: Paulist Press, 1989), 26.

[224] Ontario Catholic Directory: 1972, Toronto: Newman Foundation of Toronto. Canadian Catholic Church Directory: 1992, Montreal: B.M. Advertising, Inc.

Father Ryan's Response to Change

We may now explore Father Ryan's reaction to the changes that had taken place in Catholic education and in women's religious life in Ontario, a response most concretely manifested in the founding of the Sisters of Our Lady Immaculate.

Following the publication of the Canadian Catechism in 1972 and with the permission of Bishop Reding, Father Ryan wrote a letter to the Evaluation Committee for the Canadian Catechism series. The thoughts expressed in this letter summarize the problems with catechetics which Father Ryan wanted to see rectified.

> I hear good teachers complaining over and over again that there is very little religious content in the text they are asked to use. They are of the opinion that if this series alone is the source of the material to be taught to the children, the result will be that the children, after eight years of this type of religious instruction, will know practically nothing about the Catholic Faith....Perhaps the greatest danger arising from the use of this series is that wrong attitudes are subtly fostered. Matters of the utmost importance to a Catholic child are but briefly treated. This can only create in the child's mind

the notion that they are not important....There is far too much at stake – the Faith of our children – for us to make the mistake of continuing to use this type of religion text....From my perspective, I believe that the simplest and most effective solution is to quietly discontinue the use of this series in our schools. It will not be difficult to find another series which combines solid pedagogical principles, modern techniques and doctrinal content.[225]

Father Ryan felt that each bishop had to muster the courage to root out the catechetical establishment that had become entrenched by the mid-1970s, to order a new reliable catechetical series for use in his diocese, and to insist that the Catholic faith be taught in all the Catholic schools in his diocese. He wrote "It fills me with sadness to see how ignorant most of our children are in matters of Faith – from the youngest to the oldest." He expressed himself plainly to Bishop Reding on the subject "because I believe that the Religious education of our children is so important and because I believe that we have taken a back seat and permitted Religious Consultants, directors, text-

---

[225] DHA, letter from Father Ryan to Evaluation Committee for the Canadian Catechism, February 25, 1974, file P36-007-006.

book authors etc. to take over – and I think they are not doing a good job."[226]

Ryan also deeply regretted some of the developments he witnessed with respect to the renewal of religious life. He perceived that women religious risked losing their identity as persons consecrated to Christ as they abandoned their hierarchical structure, their community life and prayer and their shared apostolate.[227] He felt that sisters ought to maintain the habit as an external sign of their consecration,[228] "so that everyone will recognize Sister. Our Catholic people love to see their nuns dressed as nuns, and they want to cherish and honour them, and to know that they are living lives dedicated entirely to our Lord."[229] Father Ryan also regretted the fact that sisters were leaving their teaching posts in the Catholic school system, which decision, as we have seen, was the result of many cultural and ecclesial shifts.

Ryan felt that something had to be done to promote and preserve the identity of consecrated religious and the accurate transmission of the faith to

---

[226] DHA, Sisters of Our Lady Immaculate file, letter from Father Ryan to Bishop Reding, September 7, 1973, file P36.002.006.

[227] Sister Joan McMahon, CSJ, interview by John Perdue, Dundas, ON, February 6, 2013, transcript in SOLIA.

[228] SOLIA, Father Loyd Ryan. Letter to Sandra Guthmiller, March 7, 1976, Folder 'A'.

[229] Bishop Matthew Ustrzycki, interview by John Perdue, Guelph, ON, December 29, 2011, recording in SOLIA.

young people. He was not alone in this sentiment; Ryan conferred with several like-minded parishioners at the Church of Our Lady in Guelph and with brother priests who shared his concerns. [230] Among his confidants were Dorothy Beitz, Irene Smith and Carol Mary Awry.[231] Carol and Dorothy were catechists and members of the Legion of Mary at the Church of Our Lady where Father Ryan was stationed.[232] From these meetings it was decided over the summer of 1975 that an attempt ought to be made to found a new congregation of women religious with a two-fold purpose; (1) to provide young Catholic women with an avenue for achieving sanctity by living a traditional religious life;[233] and (2) to ensure the complete and

---

[230] Mother St. Henry Moloney, SOLI, interview by John Perdue, Cambridge, ON, November 20, 2009, recording in SOLIA; Carol Mary Awry, memories of Father Ryan mailed to John Perdue, December, 2012, SOLIA. Among the priests Father Ryan communicated with was Father Oliver Moloney (1920-2005) of the Archdiocese of Toronto.

[231] SOLIA, Carol Mary Awry, memories of Father Ryan mailed to John Perdue, December, 2012.

[232] Ibid. While little information is available on Ms. Dorothy Beitz, her letters reveal her to be a strong woman with deep faith. She was a former Catholic schoolteacher, and had, in her younger years, desired to enter the Sisters of Service, but had been denied entry on account of a hearing impairment. Dorothy clearly had a profound love for religious life. SOLIA, Folder 'A'.

[233] Bishop John-Michael Sherlock, telephone interview by John Perdue, Peterborough, ON, March 26, 2012, transcript in SOLIA.

accurate transmission of the Catholic faith to schoolchildren.[234] Ryan's great hope was that the sisters, by combining a profound contemplative life with an active teaching apostolate, would play a role in ensuring the Catholic education of youth.[235] Because he was able to obtain the support of bishop Reding, it was decided that, should there be interested women, the congregation would start at the Church of Our Lady in Guelph as soon as possible.[236] The sisters, it was imagined, would reside in what had been the caretaker's house before his retirement in 1977, but the house had first to be renovated to accommodate a small number of sisters and a chapel.[237]

The Sisters of Our Lady Immaculate

The first public manifestation of Father Ryan's efforts at establishing a religious order speaks clearly to the approach he would follow – it was

---

[234] DHA, Sisters of Our Lady Immaculate file, letter from Bishop Reding to Sister Teresa Ann, March 10, 1977, file P36.007.007.

[235] Mother St. Henry Moloney, SOLI, interview by John Perdue, Cambridge, ON, November 20, 2009, recording in SOLIA.

[236] DHA, Sisters of Our Lady Immaculate file, letter from Father Ryan to Bishop Reding, July 7, 1977, file P36.007.007.

[237] Ibid.

simple and straightforward, and it was supported by his Ordinary. [238] It came in the form of an advertisement in *the Catholic Register* on August 30, 1975[239] entitled "Vocation Call".

Editor:

A group of people recently gathered at Guelph, Ontario, to discuss two very vital problems of the Church. First – the small number of women who are entering Religious life; and second – the desperate and widespread need of good teachers of Religion. Those attending the meeting felt that God is calling more young women to Religious life, and that many of these vocations are being lost. In order to solve this vexing problem, it was decided to explore the possibility of establishing a new Religious Group or Community for young women. The basic and continuing purpose of this community must be to develop a strong spiritual life – through devotion to Our

---

[238] As mentioned, Father Ryan had consulted with Bishop Paul Reding and received his permission to proceed in his endeavor to found a new religious community. "I have given him permission to explore the possibility of such a foundation." DHA, Sisters of Our Lady Immaculate file, letter from Bishop Reding to Sr. Lucille Martin, April 30, 1979.

[239] The advertisement was re-published in the *Register* on October 26, 1975.

Lord in the Blessed Sacrament; devotion to our Blessed Mother; a striving for holiness of life; for a discarding of worldliness by prayer, penance and poverty for life. Besides this primary purpose of sanctity and union with God, the secondary purpose would be to strive to become capable teachers of Religion, acquiring a thorough knowledge of our Holy Faith, its doctrines, practices, and rich traditions and being instructed in the best methods of teaching and passing on this Faith to our children. Interested readers are asked to write to: Miss Irene Smith, P.O. Box 298, Belle River, Ontario, Canada. Or to: Miss Dorothy Beitz, 83 Durham St., Guelph, Ontario, Canada. We are particularly anxious to hear from any young woman or girl who feels that she may be called to such a life as we briefly described.

(Miss) Dorothy Beitz
Guelph, Ontario[240]

The names of Miss Dorothy Beitz and Miss Irene Smith appear on the advertisement above. In typically self-effacing fashion, Father Ryan had asked these

---

[240] See Appendix J for another version of this advertisement.

women to affix their names to the article rather than his.[241] In subsequent months, Ryan and his confidants strove to publish their advertisement in as many Catholic periodicals as possible. They succeeded in having it appear in the magazine *Leaves*, a publication of the Mariannhill Mission Society in Dearborn, Michigan,[242] in *Our Sunday Visitor*[243] and in *The Companion*, the publication of the Conventual Franciscan Friars in Toronto.[244] Unsuccessful efforts were made to have the ad published in *The Annals of Saint Anne*, a bi-monthly publication connected to the St. Anne-de-Beaupré shrine in Quebec,[245] and in *Restoration*, a publication of Madonna House in Combermere, Ontario.[246]

The responses to this advertisement were heartening – dozens of interested women wrote to

---

[241] SOLIA, Carol Mary Awry, memories of Father Ryan mailed to John Perdue, December, 2012.

[242] Dorothy Beitz, letter to the editor, *Leaves*, March-April, 1976. Confirmation that the advertisement would be published came in September, 1975. SOLIA, Father Anthony Kirschner, CMM, letter to Dorothy Beitz, September 9, 1975.

[243] Dorothy Beitz, letter to the editor, *Our Sunday Visitor*, October 26, 1975.

[244] SOLIA, Father Leo, OFM Conv., letter to Dorothy Beitz, September 4, 1975. Letter indicates that Dorothy's advertisement would be published in *The Companion of St. Francis and St. Anthony*.

[245] SOLIA, Father Bertrand Lessard, CSSR, letter to Dorothy Beitz, September 5, 1975.

[246] SOLIA, Father John Callahan, letter to Dorothy Beitz, September 17, 1975.

Dorothy Beitz from all over North America and beyond. Letters arrived from California, Texas, Michigan, Minnesota, Ontario, South Dakota, Manitoba, Quebec, Maine, and many from the Philippines.[247] Dorothy also received letters of support from men and women who were not able or interested in joining the fledgling religious community, but who nevertheless desired to show their support of the endeavour. There was a great deal of communication back and forth between Dorothy Beitz and Father Ryan; Dorothy would filter the responses and pass the more promising ones on to Father, with the respondents' permission.[248]

The young women who wrote were from all walks of life; some were just finishing high school or had Bachelor's degrees, while others were consecrated religious uncomfortable with the efforts at renewal that were being undertaken by their congregations. [249] There were certainly points of commonality between respondents, however. Four topics in particular arose repeatedly throughout the early correspondence in the establishment of the new community, and these demonstrate the concerns of interested young women.

---

[247] Letters in SOLIA.

[248] SOLIA, Folder 'A' package 'A.2'. There are many examples of notes passed between Father Ryan and Dorothy Beitz, and of letters sent to interested young women.

[249] SOLIA, Folder 'A'.

1) The desire to wear a habit as an external sign of their identity.

2) The desire to be faithful to the Magisterium of the Church.

3) The desire for a structured routine of community prayer, with time set aside for contemplation.

4) A strong interest in teaching catechism.

The most noteworthy response came from Sister Mary Josephine Mulligan, a Grey Sister of the Immaculate Conception from Pembroke, Ontario.[250] Sister Mary Josephine came to visit Father Ryan at the Church of Our Lady in Guelph in March of 1976,[251] and there was an immediate union of heart and mind between the two. Sister Josephine was uncomfortable with the rapidity of the reforms that had taken place in her own congregation, and, like Ryan, feared that women religious were losing their identities through the deterioration of their perpetual vows of poverty, chastity and obedience. She felt that what the Fathers at the Second Vatican Council had intended for the renewal of religious life had been "adulterated" in many articles and lectures.[252] She deeply desired the

---

[250] SOLIA, Dorothy Beitz, letter to Sister Mary Josephine Mulligan, GSIC, September 12, 1975, Folder 'A'.

[251] SOLIA, Father Loyd Ryan, letter to Sandra Guthmiller, March 7, 1976, Folder 'A'.

[252] Sister Mary Josephine Mulligan, "Women Religious as Educators and Evangelizers" (paper presented at the Catholics United for the Faith Congress, London, Ontario, 1978).

establishment of a community whose members would "strive for personal holiness through prayer and contemplation – with special emphasis on devotion to the Blessed Sacrament and to our Blessed Mother".[253]

From this meeting, it was decided that Sister Josephine would come to Guelph and found the new order. Before this could happen, however, she would need to be exclaustrated from the Grey Sisters of the Immaculate Conception.[254] While this process was underway,[255] the necessary provisions were made for her living quarters at the Church of Our Lady. The order was to be named after Our Lady, to whose providence Father Ryan had entrusted the whole endeavour, and in whose honour the sisters' first parish church was named. The newly renovated convent was blessed and Sister Mary Josephine moved in on August 1, 1977, officially beginning the

---

[253] Sister Mary Josephine Mulligan, *Women Religious as Educators*.

[254] "Father [Ryan] has indicated that he has had discussion with Sister and that, hopefully, she would be the start of this Religious Community." DHA, Sisters of Our Lady Immaculate file, letter from Bishop Reding to Sister Teresa Ann, March 10, 1977, file P36.007.007. Sister Teresa Ann was the Mother Superior of the Grey Nuns in Pembroke at the time of Sister Mary Josephine's exclaustration.

[255] Sister Mary Josephine travelled to Rome to deal with juridical matters pertaining to her exclaustration. Mrs. Carol Mary Awry accompanied her on this journey. Carol Mary Awry, memories of Father Loyd Ryan mailed to John Perdue, December 2012. See the Code of Canon Law, Canon 686 §1-2.

life of the *Sisters of Our Lady Immaculate*.[256] Sister Mary Josephine was able find a position as Religious Consultant for the Wellington County Separate School Board,[257] providing an important source of income for the new community.

The establishment of the Sisters of Our Lady Immaculate occasioned a beautiful synthesis of effort between a priest, a religious and a layperson, all of whom were deeply concerned with the renewal of religious life and the evangelization of Catholic youth. Throughout the foundation of the community, letters continued to be exchanged between interested young women and Father Ryan, Mother Mary Josephine and Dorothy Beitz.[258] This is a vibrant example of the

---

[256] See Appendix K for a list of significant historical and canonical developments in the life of the Sisters of Our Lady Immaculate community.

[257] DHA, Sisters of Our Lady Immaculate file, letter from Bishop Reding to Sister Teresa Ann, March 10, 1977, file P36.007.007.

[258] Father Ryan's vision, as described to Lisa, a young woman considering joining the fledgling order: "A community of Sisters whose primary goal is to love our dear Lord and to strive after holiness of life. Devotion to Our Lord in the Blessed Sacrament will be encouraged in every possible way, and devotion to Our Lady – There will be a really happy, simple community life – mutual love – a program of daily spiritual exercises, poverty – A religious habit (a nice one). We will be hoping that everyone will be trying to be a little saint – a very happy saint. The secondary purpose will be the teaching of religion. The sisters will be prepared thoroughly for this, and they will find, I am sure, that the Lord will use them as His instruments in this most important apostolic work." SOLIA,

implementation of the teachings and exhortations of Vatican II – lay people, religious and priests working together to breathe new life into communities of consecrated religious and to promote the evangelization of peoples.

Since their foundation, The Sisters of Our Lady Immaculate have made every effort to maintain and deepen their identity as consecrated religious. As Father Ryan and Mother Mary Josephine had intended, they wear a practical and beautiful habit as an exterior sign of their consecration. Their habit is grey for candidates and postulants and navy blue for novices, temporarily professed and fully professed sisters. The habit includes a veil; grey for postulants, white for novices and blue for temporarily and fully professed sisters. The sisters live a joyful community life modeled after the Rule of St. Augustine,[259] with a daily horarium including considerable time set aside for prayer. Daily attendance at Mass is at the heart of the sisters' spiritual life. They also pray the Liturgy of the Hours and find time for daily meditation, Eucharistic adoration, fifteen decades of the rosary, spiritual reading and private devotions.[260]

Father Loyd Ryan, letter to Lisa Maitland, April 20, 1976, Folder 'A'.

[259] For an explanation of the Rule of St. Augustine, see Aloysius Smith, *Explanation of the Rule of St. Augustine* (London: Sands, 1911).

[260] www.solisisters.ca.

Because Father Ryan remained a parish priest and was not a member of the new community, it was made clear from the outset that the community would be autonomous from him.[261] Thus, the community did not break up when he was moved from the Church of Our Lady Immaculate to St. Clement's parish in St. Clements in 1979. Father Ryan did, of course, take particular interest in the community's growth and wellbeing. He continued to serve as spiritual director to the SOLI community, and was especially present to the sisters during his retirement years. Besides celebrating weekly Masses, hearing confessions, offering catechesis and leading holy hours,[262] Ryan preached retreats to the sisters and to interested young

---

[261] In a letter to Sister Lucille Martin, Superior General of the Grey Sisters of the Immaculate Conception of Pembroke, Bishop Reding wrote "It is my clear understanding that Sister Mary Josephine Mulligan's present status in our diocese is a result of her response to an invitation extended by Father Lloyd Ryan (with the approval of his Bishop) to establish a new religious community in our diocese. I would want it understood that the invitation was not to establish a new religious community with Father Lloyd Ryan but to establish a new religious community. Although I am sure that Father Lloyd Ryan will always have a special interest in this foundation I can readily foresee that he will be in no way associated with same upon assignment to another parish." DHA, Sisters of Our Lady Immaculate file, letter from Bishop Reding to Sister Lucille Martin, April 30, 1979.
[262] SOLIA, Sisters of Our Lady Immaculate, *Who is the Priest?,* digital slideshow, produced by the Sisters of Our Lady Immaculate, 2003.

women who attended vocation discernment weekends.[263] He was anxious to have the sisters understand that their first and foremost mission was to conform themselves to Christ, which would lend fruitfulness to any ministry they undertook.

Today, the SOLI are twenty-two in number: eleven in perpetual vows, five in temporary profession, four novices, one postulant and one sister in perpetual profession who is in the process of transfer.[264] Their present-day convent is attached to the Marian Residence retirement home on Hillview Road in Cambridge. Several sisters are qualified teachers and others are in the process of achieving the necessary credentials. They begin their university education at Our Lady Seat of Wisdom Academy in Barry's Bay,[265] an institute that, at present, cannot independently grant bachelor's degrees. They finish their undergraduate degrees and obtain their teaching qualifications at Redeemer University College in Ancaster.[266] In keeping with the vision of their

---

[263] The SOLI archives contain file folders of sermons and retreats that Father Ryan preached for the sisters. E.g. Father Loyd Ryan, Retreat to Sisters, Oct. 7 & 8, 1993.

[264] SOLIA, Mother Dorothy Nzekwe, SOLI, email to John Perdue, May 23, 2013.

[265] http://www.seatofwisdom.org.

[266] http://www.redeemer.ca. Note that Redeemer University College is a Christian Reform school, and that the Sisters of Our Lady Immaculate are the first habited sisters with a presence on campus. The sisters have chosen to finish their degrees at Redeemer for the time being because it maintains a Christian perspective and approach.

founder, the sisters hope to start a Catholic elementary school in the near future,[267] so there is great hope that Father Ryan's catechetical vision will flourish even more powerfully soon.

In the meantime the sisters are applying for jobs with local Catholic school boards. One sister is currently teaching grade four at Holy Name of Jesus School in the Hamilton-Wentworth Catholic District School Board. The sisters also teach catechesis, prepare students for their sacraments at several parishes and run retreats for elementary and high school age students. [268] There are also several SOLI sisters who are qualified nurses or who are completing their nursing studies. These sisters are a great help to the operation of the Marian Residence, the retirement home owned and operated by the SOLI community.

The primary mission of the Sisters of Our Lady Immaculate, though, is to conform their lives to Christ through the Sacraments – primarily the Eucharist – and their lives of prayer. Father Ryan and Mother Mary Josephine, their founder and foundress, wanted nothing more than for the sisters to recognize

---

[267] Father Loyd Ryan, letter to Frank Ryan, August 24, 1993. This letter is in the possession of Mr. Tom Ryan.
[268] In 2008, the Sisters were invited by the Pastor of Blessed Sacrament Parish to run the catechetical program for the children of their parish who attend public schools. That program is presently coordinated and taught by the Sisters of Our Lady Immaculate. The pastor of St. Aloysius Parish in Kitchener asked the SOLI Sisters to undertake the same ministry in his parish in 2009 (www.solisisters.ca).

that they are the brides of Christ, called to conformity with Him. They felt called to play a role in ensuring that certain elements of traditional religious life would not be lost – a hierarchical structure, a community life and shared charism, a habit and a daily horarium with plentiful time for contemplative prayer, to name a few. Their providential meeting through the publication of an advertisement in the *Catholic Register* and the subsequent founding and flourishing of the Sisters of Our Lady Immaculate community has enabled many young women to answer the call to give themselves to Christ unreservedly. These young women were attracted to the vision of religious life – the firm awareness of their identity – that Father Ryan and Mother Mary Josephine radiated.

Conclusion

Father Loyd Ryan stands out as a pre-eminent promoter of vocations in the diocese of Hamilton and serves as an example to priests and religious who wish to foster vocations. He was a man who understood the primacy of *being* over *doing* and consequently held very strong convictions about his identity as a Catholic priest and about what it meant to be a consecrated religious. The priest, to Father Ryan, was an *alter Christus* – another Christ – meant to extend the ministry of Christ through time, primarily through the sacrifice of the Mass and the celebration of the other Sacraments. The female religious was the bride of Christ, called to an ever-deeper communion with Him through her vows of poverty, chastity and obedience. Ryan tenaciously clung to many habits, traditions and devotions that he considered important to the safeguarding of religious identity.

Ryan had a balanced, incarnational approach to his ministry; an approach that enabled either the human or the transcendent aspects of his priesthood to stand out, depending upon the cultural and ecclesial milieu. In the early years of his ministry, when young men needed to see the humanity and accessibility of the priesthood, they were drawn to Ryan's warmth and affability. In the later years of his priesthood, when aspirants to the priesthood needed to see the stability of the priesthood and its sacred dimensions, Ryan's spiritual depth and the dignity he brought to the Mass attracted attention. Young women sympathized with Ryan's vision of consecrated religious life and his concern over the efforts at renewal among religious congregations following the Second Vatican Council. These efforts had, in many instances, led to a loss of identity for many religious sisters. Several consecrated religious, notably Mother Mary Josephine Mulligan from the Grey Sisters of the Immaculate Conception in Pembroke, and many young women discerning vocations to religious life joined Ryan in his effort to found a new community of consecrated religious in the diocese of Hamilton, today known as the Sisters of Our Lady Immaculate.

Father Ryan serves as an example for those seeking to promote priestly and religious vocations in the Church today. To do so successfully, the priest or religious must strive first to deepen his or her own religious identity. He or she must, by means of prayer and Sacrament, enter into deeper communion with Christ. Once the habits, devotions and externals that help to appropriate one's identity have been personally fostered, they can be promoted among others, especially those actively discerning a call to the priesthood or to religious life. A well-formed religious identity, though, must be the source of pastoral praxis, including efforts to promote vocations.

Father Ryan once said "It is one of [the parish priest's] most important works to do his utmost to detect, encourage, and protect potential vocations to the Religious Life" and "St. Thomas Aquinas states that those who induce others to enter Religion meet a great reward."[269] It is my prayer that Father Ryan, who strove diligently to foster religious and priestly vocations in the diocese of Hamilton, will receive his reward.

---

[269] SOLIA, Folder 'A' package 'A.2'.

Appendixes

APPENDIX A
A story from Loyd's childhood

As a boy, Loyd Ryan's nephew Michael Ryan heard the story that his uncle Loyd received a miraculous healing as a young lad. It is unclear what illness Loyd suffered from, but it caused him to walk with a crutch.[270] Nephews Paul Ryan and John Quesnelle likewise have vague recollections of a story involving a miraculous healing, and speculate that Ryan may have been afflicted with polio.[271] Regardless, they all agree that Ryan and his parents made a pilgrimage to Martyr's Shrine, perhaps when Ryan was four or five years old, where he received a miraculous healing and left his crutch behind. However, Mrs. Mary Fleming, a long-time friend and neighbour to the Ryan's, whose memory was extraordinarily sharp at the time that I conducted my research, indicates that her family was closely connected to the Ryan's, and she has no recollection of such an event.[272] What's further, Martyr's Shrine did not open until 1926, at which time Ryan would have been nine years old. Finally, I

---

[270] Michael Ryan, interview by John Perdue, Waterdown, ON, May 14, 2011, transcript in SOLIA.

[271] Paul Ryan and John Quesnelle, interview by John Perdue, Waterdown, ON, May 14, 2011, transcript in SOLIA.

[272] Mary Fleming, telephone interview by John Perdue, Scarborough, ON, January 27, 2013, transcript in SOLIA.

contacted the archivist at Martyr's Shrine, Mr. Stephen Catlin, who indicated that there are some records of favours granted in the 1920s, but Ryan's name is not among them.[273] For these reasons, this story remains unconfirmed and has not been recorded in the body of the text.

---

[273] SOLIA, Stephen Catlin, email message to John Perdue, January 21, 2013.

APPENDIX B

The parishes in which Father Loyd Ryan served during his priestly ministry

City	Parish	Dates
Hamilton	Cathedral	June 1940 – September 1942
Guelph	Sacred Heart	September 1942 – August 1945
Hamilton	St. Mary's	August 1945 – July 1947
Brantford	St. Mary's	July 1947 – August 1958
Dundalk – Pastor	St. John's	August 1958 – July 1960
Markdale – Pastor	St. Joseph's	July 1960 – September 1960
Mildmay – Pastor	Sacred Heart	September 1960 – June 1965
Guelph - Pastor	Sacred Heart	June 1965 – June 1969
Guelph – Pastor	Our Lady Immaculate	June 1969 – June 1979

Figure 1: Parishes in which Father William Loyd Ryan served during his priestly ministry in the Diocese of Hamilton, ON. [274]

---

[274] DHA, Father W.L. Ryan personnel file, "Curriculum Vitae Sheet."

APPENDIX C

Memories of Mr. Bob Chesney, demonstrating the prayerfulness of Father Loyd Ryan

Bob Chesney, whose daughter joined the Sisters of Our Lady Immaculate, taking the name Sister Anne, relates a story about Father Ryan that took place while Father Ryan was vacationing at his family home in North Brant in the 1980s. It was the day of the annual reunion and Mass in North Brant, so the Church was busy and Father Ryan wanted a quiet place to pray. Bob suggested that Father visit Mrs. Yvonne Schultz, caretaker to St. Joseph's Mission Church in Cargill at that time. Father Ryan did as had been suggested, and obtained the key. A few hours later, Mrs. Schultz showed up in a state of distress at her neighbours' house (which belonged to Bob's parents), telling them that a nice man in clerical garb had asked for the keys, and must surely be up to no good since "no man, priest or bishop, would possibly spend that much time in church." Bob's father pointed out that the car was still in front of her house, so it was likely not the case that he was up to no good. Mrs. Schultz then speculated that her visitor had suffered a stroke or heart attack. As they were on their way to investigate they met Father Ryan coming out of the Church, and they all had a good laugh.[275]

---

[275] SOLIA, Bob Chesney, email to SOLI sisters, March 4, 2004.

APPENDIX D
Memories of Father Loyd Ryan's Relatives

Father Ryan's niece Mary Quesnelle remembers Father spending his holidays on the family farm in North Brant when he was associate pastor at St. Mary's in Brantford. Father would help pick raspberries, cherries and apples to make preserves, and was generally helpful around the farm.[276] Father's days began with Mass at St. Michael's, after which he would have breakfast. Then - and other nieces and nephews remember this as well - he would pray his office, walking up and down the road for what seemed like an eternity, before he would tell the kids it was time to go "fishing, hunting, boating, shooting!!" They would catch minnows from the creek in Vesta and then fish for pike on the Saugeen River. If bass was the target species, they would catch dew worms the night before on the lawn, using flashlights. Mary remembers Fr. Ryan bringing groups of altar boys up to sleep in the haymow in the barn, and they would also go fishing, hunting, boating an swimming. Mary recounts that Father Ryan and his sister, Mary Clare, would sing Irish songs in the parlour after supper – they sang well together. Father Ryan helped to get Mary into Lorretto abbey to finish her high school education.[277]

---

[276] SOLIA, Mary Quesnelle, letter to John Perdue, October 2012.
[277] Ibid.

Mary's brother Mike recalls groundhog hunting with Father Ryan and fishing for black bass, pike, trout or sturgeon. He remembers Father Ryan's eldest brother Dan having a boat and water skis. Dan lived in Detroit, but when he came for a visit he would bring his boat and put it in Silver Lake, and Father Loyd, Mary Clare and her husband Walter would water ski. Mike also remembers Father Loyd and Father Nolan hunting deer around the Greenock Swamp area west of Walkteron. Like Mary, Mike remembers Father Ryan helping around the farm, bailing hay, for example, when the season arrived.[278]

Father Ryan's niece Elizabeth Iley says that the annual pilgrimage to St. Michael's in North Brant where Father Ryan would celebrate Mass "made a significant spiritual impact on my life."[279] Indeed, Father Ryan's pleasant, joyful presence was undergirded by a profound spiritual life and life of virtue that resonated with his nieces and nephews. His niece, Mary Louanne Schreinert, remembers that Fr. Loyd "listened with his whole being when we had problems or issues" and that "he was the uncle who made sure we were all having fun."[280] Father's nephew John writes that Father Ryan "was a great role

---

[278] SOLIA, Michael Ryan, letter to John Perdue, July 2012.
[279] SOLIA, Elizabeth Iley, letter to John Perdue, May 6, 2012.
[280] SOLIA, Mary-Louanne Schreinert, letter to John Perdue, February 6, 2012.

model in every sense of the word. He was very kind, friendly and generous."[281]

One relative of Father Ryan's particularly benefitted from the intercession of Father Ryan in her life. Mrs. Anne Hughes, Father Ryan's niece, recalls a time when she and several other members of the Ryan clan were swimming at Port Albert, ON. Father Ryan had come up for the day, and had brought his housekeeper, Laura. Young Anne overestimated her swimming ability and ventured out further than she should have, quickly losing her strength and beginning to sink. Father Ryan was sitting on the beach when an uproar arose – "she's drowning, she's drowning!!" and it was reported that a young girl was way out in the lake, sinking quickly. Father Ryan immediately rushed into the water and dragged Anne to safety. Mary Clare, Father Ryan's sister, recalls the crowd thinking that Anne was dead. Father Ryan collapsed, and Mary covered him with towels. They rushed Anne to the hospital; Mary Clare remembers this because her towels went too![282] Ms. Anne Hughes has at least one reason to be grateful to Father Ryan![283]

---

[281] SOLIA, John Sampson, letter to John Perdue, September 9, 2012.
[282] Mary Clare, interview by John Perdue, Goderich, ON, November 21, 2009, recording in SOLIA.
[283] SOLIA, Anne Hughes, letter to John Perdue, October, 2011.

Dorothy Ryan, another of Father Ryan's nieces, adds memories of berry-picking with Father Ryan, as well as Father Ryan's desire that everyone should be gathered around one large table when the family ate together – "young and old! The more the merrier!"[284] Father Ryan's nephew Paul remembers late-night car rides down country roads, where sometimes Father Loyd would turn off the lights for the thrill of riding by the moonlight. Paul also records that a visit with Father usually meant you were going to meet someone new – often priests and sisters. Paul says that Father Loyd was involved in many marriages and baptisms in the Ryan family, who were blessed to have him.[285]

---

[284] SOLIA, Dorothy Ryan, letter to John Perdue, October 20, 2011.
[285] Paul Ryan, interview by John Perdue, North Brant, ON, October 24, 2012, recording in SOLIA.

APPENDIX E

Hunting and fishing stories involving Father Loyd Ryan

Ms. Doris Azzopardi was housekeeper to Father Ryan at St. Clement's Church for three years, from 1979 to 1982. Doris has many fond memories of Father. In particular, she recalls Father Ryan and his friend Father Nolan coming home from the moose hunt with a large moose, and her wondering what they would do with all that meat! She remembers another occasion when Father Ryan had come home late from hunting and had hung a goose from a joist in the cold room without telling her. Father Ryan had a good laugh when Doris screamed upon discovering something dangling from the ceiling in the cellar! She fondly recalls that "Father Ryan lived a very active life, serving God and His people. Everyone loved him and respected him for his spirituality." She remembers his sparkling blue eyes. "He was a happy person."[286]

Mrs. Gerry Grubb was housekeeper to Fr. Ryan when Father Ryan was pastor of St. Clement's Church. Gerry remembers Father Ryan being very grateful for her work and the work of a number of ladies who would clean the rectory thoroughly every spring – to say thanks, he would take the ladies fishing at a pond in Proton that Father Ryan had

---

[286] SOLIA, Doris Azzopardi, memories of Father Loyd Ryan, October 22, 2003.

stocked himself. There, they would have a pleasant afternoon of fishing and a picnic lunch.[287]

Father Ryan's niece, Mrs. Mary Quesnelle, remembers a funny hunting story involving Father Ryan. Father had come up to North Brant to go deer hunting with Father Nolan. At the time, Father Ryan had a beagle named 'Beulah,' and Beulah got onto the trail of a rabbit and got lost several concessions from the homestead. Father Ryan and Father Nolan made a few phone calls and found out where the dog was - Father Ryan walked up the driveway calling out 'Beulah, Beulah!' only to find out that the farmer's wife's name was Beulah – he came back very red in the face![288]

[287] SOLIA, Gerry Grubb, letter to the SOLI Sisters, September 19, 2003.
[288] SOLIA, Mary Quesnelle, letter to John Perdue, October, 2012.

APPENDIX F

Ryan family tombstone in Ireland

Figure 1: Ryan family tombstone in Ireland, bearing Father Loyd Ryan's name. Father Ryan is actually buried in Calvary Roman Catholic Cemetery in Walkerton, ON, but he arranged to have his name affixed to this tombstone as a proud testament to his Irish heritage.

APPENDIX G

Recounting of a miraculous healing attributed to the intercessory prayer of Father Loyd Ryan

Fred Grespan was very close to Father Ryan in the later years of his ministry, and helped extensively with the annual pilgrimage to St. Michael's Church in North Brant on the first Sunday of August.[289] As part of this pilgrimage, Father Ryan would hear confessions and celebrate Mass, after which followed an afternoon of food, music and entertainment. Fred records that at seventy-five years of age he was diagnosed with cancer of the stomach and the bowels. He received opinions from three separate doctors, all of whom confirmed the findings. Fred had Father Ryan praying for him, and he recounts how he woke up after surgery to find Father Ryan at his side. Father Ryan told Fred that the doctors had found nothing serious – no cancer, just a minor problem with the bile duct. Nine years later, in 2003, Fred wrote "I am convinced that his [Father Ryan's] intercession had ended my days of terror."[290]

---

[289] St. Michael's Church: North Brant, Ontario 1883-1983. [Hamilton]: 1983, 115.

[290] SOLIA, Fred Grespan, letter to the SOLI Sisters, undated, Folder 'A'. This letter was received shortly after Father Ryan's death, and was most likely written in 2003.

APPENDIX H
Resolutions recorded in Loyd Ryan's seminary
journal

N.B. Some Sacerdotal Safe-Guards

(1) Whenever you have to make some important judgment for yourself or others consult some older, prudent, experienced priest.

(2) Always make your meditation in the morning - you will not go wrong if you do (very true and very important).

(3) Always say your Mass every day, and very devoutly - the most important part of your priestly Office

(4) Always go to Confession every week - choose a prudent Confessor, older if possible & tell him not only your sins but also your temptations - for if you get these at their start they will not lead to anything grave.

(5) Work is the elixir of the priestly ministry - if in a country place, an excellent opportunity to write sermons on the Sunday Gospels, etc. & to study - do not go around to neighbouring parishes & bother the priests there - Keep busy yourself - souls depend on you. If in a city parish - you will be busy all the time.

(6) Re: Office - To anticipate is a wise thing. Say it preferably in the Church before the Blessed Sacrament. There is always in any parish a reason sufficient to finish it all in the morning.

(7) Recreation - Most important to relax mind. Play

tennis, ball, golf, walk - & forget everything else while you are doing this. Best to play with fellow priests. To play cards all night is very bad sense & do not do it.

Resolutions before Ordination, June 1940

(1) To be a man of <u>faith</u> - see God's work in everything you do, or think or say. It is all for Him. To seek not yourself, but God's advantage.

(2) To be <u>humble</u> - A proud priest is a contradiction in terms. For a priest is another Christ - and how could Christ be proud.

(3) To have the ideal of your priesthood always before you - for whatever else you are - How poor, & how full of faults - you are a priest & must always strive to live up to your vocation.

(4) To be <u>charitable</u> - The most important of all virtues for a priest - The words of Christ "In "<u>this</u>" shall all men know that you are my disciples, if you have love, one for another."

(5) This charity must be shown above all in the Confessional - Always remember that Penance is the Tribunal of God's "<u>Mercy</u>" - of His <u>Mercy</u> - And if you do not always show the greatest kindness, charity & sympathy, you are committing a great offense against the trust God has placed in you.

(6) Always be cheerful - Make others happy.

Resolution made during retreat of June 1938

To take as my slogan, and guiding rule of my life the words of the Blessed Virgin, which too was the rule of her whole life, namely, "Fiat mihi secundum verbum tuum", and to have this in my lips whenever a "dose" comes along. This plus a grin at all these times and realizing that this is your "dose", and God's Holy Will.

Firmness

Always be affable, kind, good-natured, cheerful and seek always to lift others up; make them happy – <u>But</u> you must never sacrifice a principle, just to please someone or make him feel good e.g. fail to correct a person out of fear of offending him when you know he should be corrected. You will be doing him more good – he will respect you more for it because you are but doing your duty.

Obedience

Humble obedience is a virtue more necessary in the priesthood than anywhere else. Look on your superiors as representatives of God, which they are, for all authority comes from God. And all the faithful too are your masters and the representatives of God, for they have the <u>right</u> to command you & demand your time & your service. You are their servant.

APPENDIX I

*Final blessing at the Mass of thanksgiving for Father
Thomas Collins*

Figure 1: Father Thomas Collins blesses the
congregation of the Church of Our Lady Immaculate
in Guelph, ON, at the conclusion of the Mass of
Thanksgiving following his ordination to the Holy
Priesthood, May 6, 1972. Pictured (left to right) are
Father Patrick Fuerth, rector of St. Peter's Seminary in
London, Father Loyd Ryan, Father Thomas Collins,
Father John Noonan, Monsignor John Newstead and
an unidentified altar server.

APPENDIX J

A second version of the advertisement that began the SOLI community[291]

Women: Are you interested in a new religious community?
The Editor:

A few people met recently in Guelph, Ont., to discuss two very serious problems in the Church – first, the small number of women who are entering religious life today, and second, the desperate and widespread need of good teachers of religion.

Those present felt that God is calling more young women to religious life, and that many of these vocations are being lost. They believe that it is very important to find a solution. They also feel that if a solution to this first problem can be found, it will prove to be a solution to the second problem also.

After much discussion and prayer for God's guidance, it was decided to explore the possibility of establishing a new religious group or community for young women. No detailed plans were formulated. But all agreed that the basic and continuing purpose of such a religious community must be to develop a strong spiritual life – through devotion to Our Lord in the Blessed Sacrament, devotion to our Blessed

---

[291] It is not clear what publication this advertisement appeared in.

Mother, a striving for holiness of life, for a discarding of worldliness by prayer, penance and poverty of life.

Besides this primary purpose of striving for sanctity and union with God, the secondary purpose would be to strive to become truly capable teachers of religion, acquiring a thorough knowledge of our Holy Faith, its doctrines and practices and rich traditions and being instructed in the best methods of passing on this Faith to our children.

These are only a few of the ideas expressed at this meeting. If any of your readers are interested in these suggestions, we would be very happy to hear from them. We are particularly anxious to hear from any young woman or girl who feels that she may be called to such a life as was briefly described above.

Finally, we ask for your prayers that, if it is God's Will, these suggestions may bear fruit, and in whatever way it may please Him.

Miss Dorothy Beitz
83 Durham Street,
Guelph, Ont.

APPENDIX K

Significant historical and juridical developments in the life of the SOLI community

- August 27, 1976: A 'Come and See' weekend for young women interested in the SOLI community is held at the new convent in Guelph.[292]

- September 1979: Kelly Anne Chesney is the first sister to join Mother Mary Josephine, taking the name Sister Anne.

- August 1980: The Sisters move into an unoccupied convent of the School Sisters of Notre Dame at 740 William Street, Preston, Ontario.[293]

- August 1986: The sisters purchase the Marian Residence retirement home at 640 Hillview Road in Cambridge, ON and begin their ministry to the elderly.[294]

- June 24, 1988: The Sisters of Our Lady Immaculate are recognized as a Private Association of Christ's Faithful by Most Rev. A.F. Tonnos in accordance with Canon 298,

---

[292] SOLIA, Father Loyd Ryan, letter to Dorothy Beitz, August 11, 1976, Folder 'A'.

[293] SOLIA, Sister Kathleen Haley, SSND, email to John Perdue, May 23, 2013.

[294] SOLIA, Mother Dorothy Nzekwe, SOLI, email to John Perdue, May 23, 2013.

299, 300 and 321-326 inclusive of the Code of Canon Law.[295]

- October 1988: Three new sisters arrive from the Owerri area of Imo State, Nigeria.[296]
- January 25, 1991: The SOLI community is officially recognized as a Public Association of Christ's Faithful by Most Rev. A.F. Tonnos, in accordance with Canon 298, 300, 301, 304- 309 and 312-320.[297]
- 1993: The SOLI community assists with catechesis at the Immaculate Heart of Mary School, a private Catholic school founded in 1993 and led by principal Dominic Posella. The school was located at 1370 Maple Grove Road, Cambridge, ON, and sought to infuse the education offered with a stronger faith element, but it did not survive.[298]

---

[295] SOLIA, Mother Dorothy Nzekwe, SOLI, email to John Perdue, August 21, 2013.

[296] These young women had read about the SOLI community in a dated newspaper. Mother Mary Josephine travelled to Nigeria to meet with their local Ordinary before their arrival in October 1988 (John Phillips, "African Violets Bloom Here," *Church in the Modern World*, February, 1989).

[297] SOLIA, Mother Dorothy Nzekwe, SOLI, email to John Perdue, August 21, 2013.

[298] SOLIA, Mary Clare, letter to SOLI community, 2003.

- 1995: The Marian Residence is renovated to include a convent and chapel and the SOLI community moves in. [299]
- June 9, 1996: Mother Mary Josephine Mulligan dies at 77 years of age on her way to Sunday Mass on the feast of Corpus Christi.
- October 16, 1996: Sister St. Henry Moloney is elected second Mother Superior of the SOLI community. Mother St. Henry had been a Grey Sister of the Immaculate Conception with Mother Mary Josephine and had left her community to join Mother Josephine in May 1981. [300] The SOLI community grows to nine sisters by 1998. [301]
- October 11, 2002: Mother St. Henry Moloney is re-elected for a second term as Mother Superior. Due to her advanced age, she resigns in April 2007 and Mother Dorothy Nzekwe is elected Mother Superior. [302]
- 2005: The SOLI community opens Our Lady Immaculate Formation House in Glen Morris,

[299] SOLIA, Mother Dorothy Nzekwe, SOLI, email to John Perdue, May 23, 2013.
[300] John Asling, "Cambridge Nuns return to traditional convent lifestyle," *The Kitchener-Waterloo Record*, August 15, 1981.
[301] Father Loyd Ryan, letter to Frank Ryan, April 3, 1998. This letter is in the possession of Mr. Tom Ryan.
[302] SOLIA, Mother Dorothy Nzekwe, SOLI, email to John Perdue, May 23, 2013.

ON for candidates and postulants. Bishop A. Tonnos blesses the house.[303]

- 2008: St. Joseph's House of Studies is opened in Barry's Bay for sisters studying at Our Lady Seat of Wisdom Academy. Although not a formally established permanent convent, SOLI sisters do reside here during the academic year, living their conventual life. They also teach catechism and help form girls from the area in the Daughters of St. Joseph sodality.[304]

- November 1994 to March 2010: The SOLI community occupies an abandoned Notre Dame convent in Port Hood, Nova Scotia, where the sisters care for the elderly and teach catechism to the children of the parish.[305]

- August 2013: Mother Dorothy Nzekwe is re-elected for a second term as Mother Superior.

---

[303] www.solisisters.ca.

[304] Ibid.

[305] SOLIA, Mother Dorothy Nzekwe, SOLI, letter to the Most Reverend Brian Dunn, Bishop of the Antigonish Diocese, March 8, 2010.

Bibliography

Archival Collections

Archives of the Sisters of Our Lady Immaculate

Diocese of Hamilton Archives
       Bishop Joseph F. Ryan Papers
       Bishop Paul F. Reding Papers
       Bishop Anthony F. Tonnos Papers
       Father William Lloyd Ryan Papers
       Mildmay-Sacred Heart File (P93)
       Sisters of Our Lady Immaculate Papers (P36)
       St. Clement's Papers (P112)

Paul Ryan, Private Collection

St. Augustine's Seminary Archives
       William Lloyd Ryan Papers

St. Jerome's College Archives
       William Lloyd Ryan Papers

Thomas Ryan, Private Collection

Articles

Mulligan, Sister Mary Josephine. "Women Religious
       as Educators and Evangelizers." Paper

presented at the Catholics United for the Faith Congress, London, Ontario, 1978.

Savage, David W. "The Attempted Home Rule Settlement of 1916." *Eire-Ireland II* (Autumn, 1967): 132-145.

———. "The Parnell of Wales has Become the Chamberlain of England: Lloyd George and the Irish Question." *Journal of British Studies* 12 no. 1 (1972): 86-102.

Books

Bacik, James J. "The Practice of Priesthood: Working Through Today's Tensions." In *Priesthood in the Modern World*, edited by Karen Sue Smith, 51-66. Franklin: Sheed and Ward, 1999.

Booth, Karen Marshall, ed. *The People Cry – 'Send us Priests': The First Seventy-five Years of St. Augustine's Seminary of Toronto, 1913-1988 Part I.* Toronto: Metro Press, 1988.

Briere, Emile. "Priests Need Priests." Combermere: Madonna House Publications, 1992.

Bruno-Jofré Rosa. "The Process of Renewal of the
    Missionary Oblate Sister, 1963-1989." In
    *Changing Habits: Women's Religious Orders
    in Canada*, edited by Elizabeth M. Smyth,
    251-252. Ottawa: Novalis, 2007.

———. *Vision and Mission: The Missionary Oblate
    Sisters*. Montreal: McGill-Queen's University
    Press, 2005.

Cameron, James. *And Martha Served: History of the
    Sisters of St. Martha.* Halifax: Nimbus, 2000.

Canadian Catholic Church Directory: 1992.
    Montreal: B.M. Advertising, Inc., 1992.

Dixon, Robert T. *Catholic Education and Politics in
    Ontario*. Vol. IV. Toronto: Catholic
    Education Foundation of Ontario, 2003.

Dobell, Richard J. *Fifty Golden Years: St. Augustine's
    Seminary, Toronto Ontario*. Toronto: Mission
    Press, 1963.

Foyster, Ken. *Anniversary Reflections: A History of
    the Hamilton Diocese (1856-1981)*. Hamilton:
    W.L. Griffin Ltd., 1981.

Hoge, Dean R., and Jacqueline E. Wenger. *Evolving
    Visions of the Priesthood: changes from*

Vatican II to the Turn of the New Century.
Collegeville, Minn.: Liturgical Press, 2003.

McKenna, Mary O. *Charity Alive: Sisters of Charity
of Saint Vincent de Paul, Halifax, 1950-1980.*
Lanham, Md.: University Press of America,
1998.

McLaughlin, Kenneth, Gerald Stortz and James Wahl,
*Enthusiasm for the Truth: An Illustrated
History of St. Jerome's University.* Waterloo:
St. Jerome's University, 2002.

Ontario Catholic Directory: 1972. Toronto: Newman
Foundation of Toronto, 1972.

Padberg, John W., S.J. "The Contexts of Comings and
Goings." In *The Crisis in Religious
Vocations: An Inside View*, edited by Laurie
Felknor, 19-31. New York: Paulist Press,
1989.

Peyton, Patrick. *All for Her; The Autobiography of
Father Patrick Peyton, C.S.C.* Garden City,
N.Y.: Doubleday, 1967.

Pfaffinger, Janet and Patricia White, *St. Clement's
Roman Catholic Parish 160 Years: 1847-
2007 and St. Clement's Roman Catholic*

Church 150 Years: 1858-2008. St. Jacobs, ON: St. Jacobs Printery, 2008.

Power, Michael. *A Promise Fulfilled: Highlights in the Political History of Catholic Separate Schools in Ontario.* Toronto: Ontario Catholic School Trustees' Association, 2002.

Smith, Aloysius. *Explanation of the Rule of St. Augustine*. London: Sands, 1911.

Smyth, Elizabeth and Linda Wicks, eds. *Wisdom Raises Her Voice: The Sisters of St. Joseph of Toronto Celebrate 150 Years*. Toronto: Sisters of St. Joseph of Toronto, 2001.

St. Michael's Church: North Brant, Ontario 1883-1983. [Hamilton], 1983.

Toups, David L., S.T.D. *Reclaiming Our Priestly Character*. Omaha: The Institute for Priestly Formation Publications, 2010.

Walker, Franklin A. *Catholic Education and Politics in Ontario Volume II*. Toronto: The Federation of Catholic Education Associations of Ontario, 1974.

Newspapers

Church in the Modern World

Leaves

Our Sunday Visitor

The Catholic Standard

The Catholic Register

The Chesley Enterprise

The Companion of St. Francis and St. Anthony

The Kitchener-Waterloo Record

The Walkerton Herald-Times

Online Resources

CBC News. "Abortion Rights: Significant Moments in Canadian History." Last modified May 30, 2013. Accessed July 31, 2013. http://www.cbc.ca/news/canada/story/2009/01/13/f-abortion-timeline.html.

Our Lady Seat of Wisdom Academy.
http://www.seatofwisdom.org.

Redeemer University College.
http://www.redeemer.ca.

Sisters of Our Lady Immaculate. www.solisisters.ca.

Vatican Radio. "2013 Pontifical Yearbook: Permanent
Diaconate Booms in Europe, U.S." News.Va:
The Vatican Today. Last modified May 13,
2013. Accessed July 20, 2013.
http://www.news.va/en/news/2013-pontifical-
yearbook-permanent-diaconate-booms.

Papal Encyclicals and Ecclesial Documents

A Catechism of Christian Doctrine. Toronto: Catholic
Truth Society of Canada, 1949.

Annuarium statisticum Ecclesiae. Libreria Editrice
Vaticana: 1976.

Catholic Church. *Catechism of the Catholic Church*.
New York: Doubleday, 1995.

Catholic Church. *Codex iuris canonici Pii X Pontificis
Maximi iussu digestus, Benedicti Papae XV*

auctoritate promulgatus. Romae: Typis
    Polyglottis Vaticanis, 1917.

Office de Catéchèse du Québec, and Catholic Church.
    The Canadian Catechism. New York: Paulist
    Press, 1972.

Pope Paul VI *Apostolicam Actuositatem.* November
    18, 1965. www.vatican.va.

———. *Gravissimum Educationis*. October 28, 1965.
    www.vatican.va.

———. *Humanae Vitae*. July 25, 1968.
    www.vatican.va.

———. *Lumen Gentium*. November 21, 1964.
    www.vatican.va.

———. *Perfectae Caritatis*. October 28, 1965.
    www.vatican.va.

———. *Presbyterorum Ordinis*. December 7, 1965.
    www.vatican.va.

———. *Sacrosanctum Concilium.* July 25, 1968.
    www.vatican.va.

Tabularum statisticarum collectio. Vatican Press:
    1971.

Theses

Bondy, Renee D. "Roman Catholic Women Religious and Organizational Reform in English Canada: The Ursuline and Holy Names Sisters in the Diocese of London, Ontario, 1950-1970." PhD diss., University of Waterloo, 2007. Accessed July 15, 2013. http://uwspace.uwaterloo.ca/bitstream/10012/3029/1/Dissertation&20-%Renee%20Bondy.pdf.

36275863R00080

Made in the USA
Charleston, SC
29 November 2014